THE
SNOWY OWL
SCIENTIST

A male snowy owl carries a brown lemming to his nest, where one of his chicks will eagerly consume it.

THE
SNOWY OWL
SCIENTIST

TEXT AND PHOTOS BY
MARK WILSON

CLARION BOOKS

An Imprint of HarperCollins*Publishers*

BOSTON   NEW YORK

**For my parents, Faith and Frank, who
instilled in me a love for wild places and
the plants and animals who live there**

Clarion Books is an imprint of HarperCollins Publishers.
The Snowy Owl Scientist
Copyright © 2022 by Mark Wilson
All photographs © 2022 by Mark Wilson except the following photographs and images:
Daniel Cox: pp. 20 (right), 52, 54 (left), 55, 66, 68 (left and right), 69; Claire Emery: pp. 26, 28 (top
and bottom); David Hastings: diagram p. 13; Denver Holt: p. 17; Raymond MacDonald: p. 73;
Gordon Morrison: owl tracks pp. i and 87; Owl Research Institute: pp. 18, 20 (map, left), 62
Maps © 2022 by Sean McNaughton
clarionbooks.com
Library of Congress Cataloging-in-Publication Data has been applied for.
ISBN: 978-0-358-32959-6
The text was set in Adobe Garamond and Avenir Next.
Interior design by Nina Simoneaux
Manufactured in Italy
RTLO 10 9 8 7 6 5 4 3 2 1
4500842943
First Edition

CONTENTS

This young snowy owl will soon migrate southward, perhaps reaching Washington State or Montana, where she will overwinter.

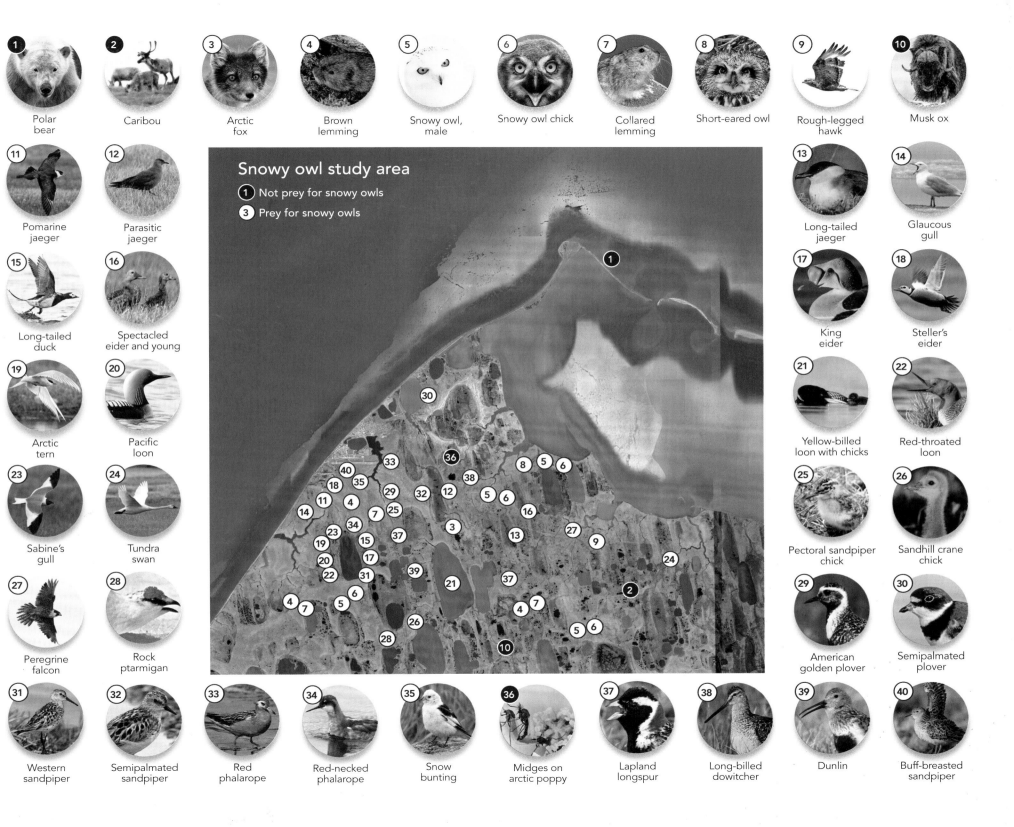

Snowy owl study area

1 Not prey for snowy owls
3 Prey for snowy owls

1. Polar bear
2. Caribou
3. Arctic fox
4. Brown lemming
5. Snowy owl, male
6. Snowy owl chick
7. Collared lemming
8. Short-eared owl
9. Rough-legged hawk
10. Musk ox
11. Pomarine jaeger
12. Parasitic jaeger
13. Long-tailed jaeger
14. Glaucous gull
15. Long-tailed duck
16. Spectacled eider and young
17. King eider
18. Steller's eider
19. Arctic tern
20. Pacific loon
21. Yellow-billed loon with chicks
22. Red-throated loon
23. Sabine's gull
24. Tundra swan
25. Pectoral sandpiper chick
26. Sandhill crane chick
27. Peregrine falcon
28. Rock ptarmigan
29. American golden plover
30. Semipalmated plover
31. Western sandpiper
32. Semipalmated sandpiper
33. Red phalarope
34. Red-necked phalarope
35. Snow bunting
36. Midges on arctic poppy
37. Lapland longspur
38. Long-billed dowitcher
39. Dunlin
40. Buff-breasted sandpiper

CHAPTER 1
GEAR UP!

"Everything is harder in the Arctic," says the snowy owl researcher Denver Holt. He's standing in the entryway of his rented apartment, pulling on his heavy parka with a fur-trimmed hood, thick rubber hip boots, double-layered mittens, and knit hat as he dresses for work. The calendar says July 4. Outside it feels like March back at Denver's home in Montana.

He's not complaining, just stating a fact. Getting dressed for an outdoor foray takes longer when you are on Alaska's North Slope, in the Arctic town of Utqiagvik. Especially when you drive an all-terrain vehicle into a 38-degree Fahrenheit (3-degree C.) morning with a sharp wind off the Chukchi Sea.

Denver lumbers out the door, throws his loaded daypack onto his ATV, and fires up the engine. Gravel crunches under the big knobby balloon tires as he rolls up Uula Street. We're heading out for a day of surveying

← Denver Holt, dressed warmly for driving an ATV into a far corner of his study area in the Arctic.

snowy owl nests, or the nests of *ukpik*, as the Inupiat call snowy owls. (Lucky me—I get to accompany Denver on his rounds and capture the photographs you see in this book.)

We drive past a few Inupiat, standing by their houses, wearing T-shirts or at most a long-sleeved shirt. This is summer for residents, who have endured a long, sunless winter of subzero temperatures and lots of wind. They know what real cold is, and on this morning it's nowhere to be found.

I follow the dust plume Denver's ATV kicks up, driving a beat-up rented pickup truck with window cranks that don't work and a windshield wearing a spiderweb of cracks. Gravel roads in the Arctic get to your windshield sooner or later.

We head south out of town and the road soon passes through a sweep-to-the-horizon plain of grasses, sedges, lichens, and ground-hugging flowers. From a distance, tundra looks like an endless lumpy lawn, with mounds mushrooming up here and there. Hidden several inches (several centimeters) below the plant life is frozen soil called permafrost. Trees

→ A pomarine jaeger calls a shrill warning to humans walking through its nesting territory.

↑ Snowy owl researcher Denver Holt gets buzzed by a defensive pomarine jaeger.

don't grow here. Cold, windy winters restrict plants from growing upward, keeping them low, creeping and stunted.

We park on the shoulder of a hardly maintained gravel road with numerous ruts cradling expansive puddles. Denver dismounts his ATV as if he's getting off a horse. He hoists his pack and we step off the roadbed onto soft tundra in an area called Ukpeagvik, which translates to the place where snowy owls are hunted.

Walking this terrain is easy on the knees but tough on the leg muscles. It's kind of like walking across a giant sponge in slow motion while wearing big boots—slightly bouncy, fun, and tiring all at the same time. Add water to the tundra sponge and the walking turns to slogging: slower yet and even more tiring. But still fun.

We are about to cross the territory of a pair of nesting pomarine jaegers (pronounced "YAY-gur")—big, powerful, fast-flying birds that resemble a cross between a gull and a hawk. They have a dark cap that looks like an executioner's hood. And as we soon learn, it's an apt fashion statement, that dark cap: The jaegers don't want us in their nesting territory. Here comes one now!

EEURRR-EEURRR-EEURRR, warns the jaeger, shrilly. At least we can hear him coming. Denver ducks as the jaeger veers at him then peels away at the last second. But the barrel-chested male comes at us again, this time from behind. Denver keeps

Optical Tools of a Snowy Owl Researcher

Find Denver traipsing the tundra or rolling across the wide-open landscape on his ATV and you'll notice pair of binoculars hanging from his neck or shoulder. He favors the 10-power version. That means snowy owls appear ten times closer when viewed through the binoculars than if Denver viewed them with his naked eyes.

Denver's binoculars are 10x40mm. In conversation you would say he uses "ten-by-forty" binoculars. The first number is the power or magnification. The second number denotes the diameter, in millimeters, of the front lenses. The larger the second number is, the more light binoculars can gather. However, the larger that front lens gets, the heavier the binoculars become. The 10x50mm or 10x60mm binoculars can feel like a heavy brick hanging off your neck, especially toward the end of a long day on the tundra.

Field researchers, naturalists, and birders use binoculars that offer a useful compromise between magnification, light-gathering ability, and weight. Ten-power binoculars are best suited for experienced users. A beginning birder will find 7- or 8-power binoculars easier to hold steady and more comfortable to use. The 7x35 or 8x40 binoculars are great for newbies. Close-focus models (focusing down to five or six feet, or less than two meters) are useful for studying details of nearby plants, birds, or insects.

To search wide swaths of tundra for nesting owls, Denver uses his binoculars for sweeping views. When he needs extreme magnification of a distant detail (think: Is that a glaucous gull or a snowy owl nesting on that mound a mile away?), he hauls a spotting scope from his ATV's storage compartment. His scope has a zooming eyepiece that can magnify distant birds by twenty to forty-five times. Denver mounts the scope on a tripod to hold it steady. This reduces eye-fatiguing vibrations caused by shaking hands or wind.

Denver scans the tundra first with binoculars (left) and then with a 15–45x60mm spotting scope (above) to locate nesting snowy owls. Scanning with optics saves Denver the huge effort of having to walk scores of miles (kilometers) across his study area.

Hand-holding a spotting scope is a recipe for eye strain and headaches.

There's one more, lesser-known use for binoculars: If you look through the large end, the tool functions as a magnifying glass for small things in your hand, say an owl pellet, a feather, a small bone, a seed, or an insect part.

Could Denver do his work without these optical tools? Not well. These optical aids save Denver loads of time and effort in locating his far-flung study subjects.

walking, covering his head with both of his gloved hands.

The jaeger swings wide and rapidly approaches a third time. He speeds in, sure-winged and fearless, and bops Denver on his crown.

"Whose idea was it to come this way?" he asks rhetorically. (It was mine, and next time we visit this particular snowy owl nest, Denver picks a route that avoids the jaegers' territory so as not to disturb them.)

The jaegers are robust and energetic. Their strong defense of their nesting territory shows they are good parents. Their well-protected chicks will have a good chance at making it to fledging.

In half a minute more, the male's mate leaves the distant nest and joins the fray, and now we have *two* upset jaegers flying at us from front and back.

EEURRRR-EEURRR-EEURRR-EEURRR-EEURRR, they whine in harmony, using high-pitched, irritated voices. They can't wait for us to leave their territory, and neither can we. We push onward, soon leaving the jaegers to their chick-rearing duties.

Denver turns his eyes to the horizon, where a distant white speck stands upright. It's a male snowy owl, and Denver watches him through his 10-power binoculars as the owl watches us.

At a snowy owl nest, it's always the female that incubates the eggs or broods the chicks. The male will stand off a bit from the nest, sometimes as sentry, or sometimes he's a great distance away, hunting.

Male snowy owls are whiter than females, often seeming to shine almost as brightly as fresh snow. Females' feather markings are darker (and there are more of them). Their feathers are also often soiled from the rigors of nesting. An experienced observer easily tells the males from the females on the breeding grounds.

We plod closer.

Denver's scrutinizing gaze moves off the male owl. He studies a sliver of white on top of a tundra mound, a female snowy owl lying prone on her eggs or chicks. We have come to see which it is—eggs or chicks.

We trudge a few hurried steps more and the distant spot of white lifts off from the mound.

"The first line of nest defense for snowy owls is the female leaves the nest," says Denver. If she vacates the nest while a potential predator is at a considerable distance, it would have a harder time finding her chicks or eggs.

Denver starts counting his paces. He will note the distance at which the female flew, or flushed, from the nest. Denver notes flushing distances of all the females at nests in his study area—another set of data to better define snowy owl behavior.

Next, the male owl takes flight, angling our way.

Are we about to be attacked by another defensive father protecting his youngsters?

Kind of. The male flies out to meet us when we are still several hundred yards (meters) from the nest. He circles us, barking sharply as he glides on gleaming white wings. Denver doesn't seem worried. He knows that this male doesn't strike human intruders who wander into his nesting territory. Usually.

We approach the grassy mound, unremarkable in appearance from forty paces and looking like scores of other mounds scattered across the tundra, now that the female has left it. We draw near. Denver pulls off his mittens and knit cap and lays them at the edge of the nest, forming a soft wind block for the inhabitants.

A newly hatched chick and four eggs gleam white from the nest. The chick can't be more than a day or two old, as its eyes aren't open yet, but already he or she wears a thin coat of fine white down.

An egg next to the chick shows two star-shaped cracks, as if someone had smacked it with a tiny hammer. An unhatched chick works from within to smash its way out of the imprisoning shell. The chick's eggshell escape could take up to two days of exhausting work. Holding our ears close to the egg, we hear faint peeps coming from the chick inside.

Denver carefully lies down next to the nest bowl, a shallow depression on top of the mound. Molted white body feathers from the mother encircle the eggs and chick. Denver's

↑ A newly hatched snowy owl chick rests its head on eggs in the nest. Note that the egg closest to the camera has a small web of cracks in it—evidence that a chick inside the egg is working to smash its way out.

face hovers over the family scene, checking to see that the tiny chick is okay and that all is fine with the eggs. Only a few bits of bloody shell remain in the nest bowl from the chick's hatching. One of the adults must have carted off the rest. In previous summers, Denver weighed the chick and measured the eggs, but after years of taking such measurements, he has gathered enough data to write a paper on snowy owl egg and chick development.

However, Denver pulls out a small spring scale to weigh a dead brown lemming (a small rodent that makes up 95 percent of a snowy owl's summer diet) left on the nest rim. He scribbles a few notes in a field notebook.

"Okay. We need to go," Denver abruptly announces. We've been at the nest no more than two to three minutes, but without their mother's warmth, young chicks and eggs can get cold quickly. Denver pulls his hat and mittens back from the nest rim and puts them on. Then we hustle away from the nest so the mother can return to her duties of incubating and brooding and the father can go back to hunting for lemmings for his mate and their newly hatched chick.

From afar, we take one last look through binoculars to confirm that the female is back on the nest. She's doing what she knows is best—hunkering over her family, keeping them protected and warm.

Snowy owls are one of the few owl breeds that construct a nest, though the nest is just a shallow depression scraped out atop a grassy mound and lined with a few grasses and maybe some lichens. Denver has found through years of observation that snowy owls usually lay from four to eight eggs.

A brooding snowy owl mother will center an area of bare skin on her belly, called a brood patch, over the chick and eggs. She lowers the brood patch onto her family, quickly warming them while protecting them from cutting winds, rain, and sleet showers.

Away from the nest, we hear the whining *EEURRR-EEURRR-EEURRR* of a pomarine jaeger. But this time the jaeger is not heading our way. Instead, he's making wide, sweeping dives at the male snowy owl, who is standing on the tundra.

Each time, as the jaeger passes close, the owl leaps up with his talons splayed upward in an attempt to grab the harassing jaeger. Strangely, the owl closes his eyes midleap, leap after leap, while the jaeger is unblinking its attack. After several more harassing dives, the jaeger breaks off the skirmish and flies back to his mate at their nest. The male snowy owl returns to his hunt for lemmings.

Because their nesting territories abutted, this male snowy owl often tangled with a defensive male pomarine jaeger. Each bird views the other as a potential predator of their eggs and chicks. Additionally, both birds potentially compete for the same lemmings, an important staple in their summer diet.

CHAPTER 2
THE NOMADS ARRIVE

Every spring snowy owls gather at Ukpeagvik, a special swath of coastal Alaskan tundra, to scrape out nests on snow-covered mounds, lay their white eggs, and raise their fuzzy gray chicks. The Inupiat once hunted *ukpik* here, eating it when seal or whale meat wasn't available. For millenia, snowy owls have gathered here to nest and raise families.

Fourteen thousand years ago, glaciers buried much of Alaska, Canada, and the northern United States under deep layers of ice. Running contrary to the widespread glaciation, much of northwestern Alaska, including the land the town of Utqiagvik now occupies, remained glacier-free.

Genetic studies suggest that snowy owls diverged from a related species of owl about four million years ago. While evidence is hard to come by, snowy owls probably have come to Ukpeagvik to nest for many thousands of years, most likely pre-dating human settlement.

Arriving centuries or millennia after snowy owls, Inupiat families settled the area roughly four thousand years ago, perhaps attracted by the greening summer tundra and easy access to abundant marine mammals to hunt. On occasion, these subsistence hunters would kill a snowy owl to eat, or perhaps sew a bag or pouch from its skin. But mostly these early hunters would hunt caribou, seals, and whales.

Fast forward to today. The glaciers that once covered most of Alaska and Canada have retreated, and now they only hang on in the coolness of mountains.

But Ukpeagvik still attracts snowy owls to come and nest. Built on edge of Ukpeagvik is the northernmost town in the United States, Utqiagvik. Located more than 300 hundred miles (483 kilometers) north of the Arctic Circle, the town sits alone on the tundra, situated at the western edge of Alaska's North Slope. The North Slope is the only area in Alaska or the

← The Utqiagvik community comes together in late June, celebrating the end of the spring whaling season with a traditional blanket toss. Using a blanket made from walrus hide, the toss originally was used to loft a hunter so he could spot game on the distant horizon.

A male snowy owl checks out researchers traversing his nesting territory.

other forty-nine states where snowy owls regularly nest and raise their chicks. The Slope has the right mix of coastal, low-elevation tundra and a rich presence of lemmings and nesting birds who are potential meals for hungry snowy owl families.

Beneath the land, large deposits of natural gas are tapped by gas wells. An intricate network of high-pressure pipelines stilts across the tundra, bringing the gas to town for heat and electricity. The pipes frequently serve as perches for hunting snowy owls.

The North Slope happens to be the only area in North America where Natives are legally allowed to hunt snowy owls. The Inupiat don't hunt them much anymore, though, as the community realizes how special the owls' presence is, attracting positive attention for the community from tourists and researchers.

Tourists tend toward short stays in Utqiagvik. Their best chance to see a snowy owl comes when one perches on a roadside power pole or peaked roof on the edge of town. Few tourists have the time, knowledge, equipment, or permits needed to venture far onto the tundra where a snowy owl pair might be nesting. So snowy owls often elude visitors' eyes, but perhaps the mere possibility of seeing an owl fuels their hopeful visits.

As for other tundra-treading researchers, Denver strives to educate them on how snowy owl females flush from the nest upon seeing a human, exposing their eggs and chicks to the cold. Waterfowl and shorebird researchers travel far afield, conducting nesting surveys. Their forays are the ones most likely to bring them into a snowy owl nesting territory. And since there is yearly turnover among field researchers, Denver faces a new group to educate every summer.

Formerly named Barrow, the town of Utqiagvik looks over the Beaufort Sea to the north and northeast and the Chukchi

Sea to the west. Together the seas form the Arctic Ocean.

Permanently frozen earth underlies Utqiagvik. In places, this permafrost penetrates 600 to 800 feet (183 to 244 meters) deep. Some five thousand people, mostly Inupiat, call Utqiagvik home. In days long past, the Inupiat built turf houses on the tundra here, the roofs supported by bowhead whale rib bones. Those old shelters crumbled back into the land long ago.

Today, modern wooden houses in Utqiagvik perch on pilings so that the permafrost under them won't thaw, which in turn prevents the houses from sinking into the earth.

Utqiagvik's high school football team, the Whalers, plays on blue and yellow artificial turf on a chain-link-fenced field just north of town, within view of the Arctic Ocean. The team hosts the only high school football games in the world where spectators and players keep one eye on the action and one eye peeled for curious polar bears who might wander up the adjacent beach and peer over the fence.

To reach Utqiagvik from outside Alaska, one must travel by plane or, rarely, boat. If you are a Native coming to town from a small Alaskan Inupiat village in winter, you might travel 60 miles (96 kilometers) or more by snow machine. No roads connect Utqiagvik to other communities.

Viewed from the air, Utqiagvik looks like a remote island of buildings floating on stilts over a large, wet, rolling lawn of grasses, flowers, lichens, and low willows. Hundreds of shallow tundra ponds dot the landscape, their waters trapped on the surface by the underlying permafrost.

In March, when wind-packed snow blankets the land and ice grips the ocean, polar bears stalk seals hauled out on the sea ice. Snowy owls also venture out to hunt sea ducks swimming in openings in the ice.

In April and May, Inupiat hunters launch slim boats through leads in the ice to hunt bowhead whales that are migrating

↑ A male long-billed dowitcher flies over tundra where his chicks are hiding. Snowy owls prey on shorebirds, particularly their downy chicks.

↑ An adult American golden plover is a strikingly beautiful shorebird that nests on the dry tundra around Utqiagvik.

↑ The gold-spangled feathers of American golden plover chicks keeps them well camouflaged at their tundra nest.

offshore. Seal, whale, and caribou hunts are traditions that run deep in this indigenous community of hunters.

Female snowy owls—hunters of a feathered kind—arrive in late spring, when snow still covers the land and sea ice covers the ocean, tightly embracing the beach. Late spring looks wintry, especially if you have traveled from a warm place in the south.

Some male snowy owls overwintered here, enduring nearly three months of twenty-four-hour darkness, subzero temperatures, and bitter Arctic winds. They've secured their nesting territories against other, later-arriving male snowy owls.

Early May in Utqiagvik sees the sun climb into the sky to shine twenty-four hours a day for the next three months. The snowy owl males that wintered here in the dark shift from a nocturnal life to a diurnal life, hunting and sleeping in twenty-four-hour daylight. Human visitors from places where nights are dark often find it difficult to sleep through the sunlit nights of an Arctic summer.

Every year since 1992, Denver Holt has traveled to Utqiagvik in early to mid-June, migrating from his home in Charlo, Montana. Denver founded the Owl Research Institute (ORI) in 1991, an organization he still oversees, working as its senior researcher.

In Montana, Denver and ORI researchers conduct multiyear studies of great gray owls, long-eared and short-eared owls, northern pygmy owls, northern hawk owls, boreal owls, and several other owl species. Some of their research projects are among the longest running owl studies in the world. But it's the snowy owl and the brown lemming, both indicator species in ORI's Arctic field research, that signify what's happening in the tundra ecosystem. Snowy owls and lemmings lure Denver back to Ukpeagvik each summer.

For two to three months, he lives in an apartment in Utqiagvik. His study area encompasses the town and a big, roughly triangular 100-square-mile (161-square-kilometer) patch of tundra that sweeps out to the south and east. When

↑ A semipalmated sandpiper chick stays hidden in tundra grasses to avoid predation by a snowy owl or pomarine jaeger.

Denver walks out his door, he's in his study area, conveniently close to nesting snowy owls.

Twenty-four-hour daylight follows him on his frequent data-gathering tramps across the tundra. From waterfowl researchers Denver heard reports of a possible snowy owl nest in a remote part of his study area. He spent long hours hiking and searching as the afternoon grew warm. His wide-ranging search revealed no nesting owls.

Tilting Toward the Seasons

The earth currently tilts 23.4 degrees from its orbital plane around the sun. That tilt is slowly decreasing. The tilt changes over time because the earth wobbles on its axis, pulled by gravity from the sun, moon, and other planets.

Places on earth that lie north of the Arctic Circle (an imaginary line that's parallel to the equator and encircles the globe at roughly 66.5608 degrees N) experience twenty-four-hour daylight in the summer because the earth tilts toward the sun.

Come winter, our planet's tilt angles land north of the Arctic Circle away from the sun, resulting in twenty-four-hour darkness. Utqiagvik lies at 71.2906 degrees N, placing it 320 miles (515 kilometers) north of the Arctic Circle.

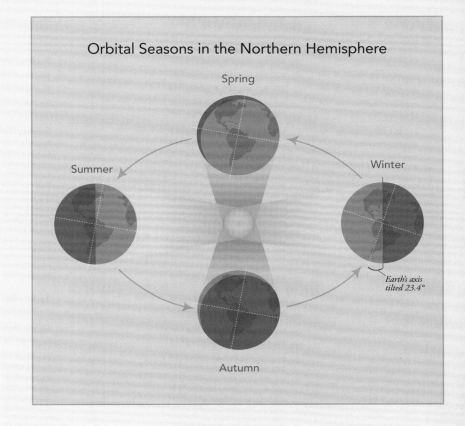

Orbital Seasons in the Northern Hemisphere

Spring

Summer

Winter

Earth's axis tilted 23.4°

Autumn

The mild afternoon enticed Denver to steal a nap from the day, as the wind had dropped and the mosquitoes weren't biting. He bedded on one of the tundra's countless mounds, the same kind of place you might spy a napping snowy owl when they use the lee of a hillock as a windbreak. Only at the sound of an approaching band of caribou did Denver awaken.

Most days, Denver's tundra companions are chilling winds, a few mosquitos, countless midges (non-biting flies), lots of lemmings, and hundreds of nesting birds. These range from Sabine's gulls to pomarine jaegers, rough-legged hawks

↑ Caribou running on the tundra could potentially trample a snowy owl's nest.

to peregrine falcons, white-fronted geese to tundra swans, Steller's eiders to king eiders, short-eared owls to sandhill cranes, Lapland longspurs to snow buntings.

Don't overlook the mind-boggling variety of shorebirds that come to nest on the tundra, some that migrate from as far away as South America. Long-billed dowitchers, American golden plovers, semipalmated sandpipers, pectoral sandpipers: All race the season to court, mate, lay eggs, and shepherd fast-growing chicks to fledging before the winter returns.

And that's just some of the birds. Don't forget the mammals: brown and collared lemmings, shrews, weasels, arctic foxes, caribou, polar bears (along the coast), and the occasional musk ox and wolf.

This amazing assemblage of creatures involuntarily makes a tundra buffet for the Arctic's most iconic avian predator. If they choose, snowy owls can catch and eat most of them (except caribou, musk ox, polar bear, and wolf).

Though snowy owls and lemmings are his study subjects,

↑ Luckily for Denver Holt and other researchers afoot on inland tundra, polar bears usually stick to the coast, where they scavenge whale and seal carcasses.

Denver recognizes the geology, climate, plants, insects, birds, and mammals that form the web of life inhabiting the tundra. He's an owl researcher first, but well-rounded naturalist comes a close second.

A Scientist in the Field

Denver enjoys fieldwork. Long ago he decided that he didn't want to spend his working life inside, stationed behind a desk or lab bench. As a college student pondering his future, Denver saw how academic positions at universities and positions at fish and wildlife agencies usually led to desk jobs with little chance to work in the field. Denver also knew that his chances of landing a job with Montana Fish, Wildlife, and Parks or the United States Fish and Wildlife Service would be slim, since there would be fierce competition for a few job postings.

Denver wanted to work outside, observing wildlife and gathering data. His early interests veered to grizzly bears, and wolves particularly. But these species had long been studied by a legion of Montana biologists. Getting a foothold in those crowded fields of wildlife biology would be tough. Denver needed to find a niche.

By his own admission, Denver was a lousy high school student, but a talented athlete who excelled at varsity football, basketball, and baseball. Classes in science and math at Belmont (Massachusetts) High School held little interest for him.

Nancy Claflin, who would ultimately be a major influence on Denver, was an avid birder and naturalist living in Belmont. After an inauspicious first meeting, she became a mentor and avid supporter of the young student.

As a high school student, Denver had sneaked into a wildlife sanctuary that abutted his high school's fields and built a rough fort in the woods to hang out in with his friends, sometimes cutting classes to do so.

When his fort was discovered by school staff, Nancy (who was on the board of the sanctuary), became aware of Denver. She met the young man and said if he needed a job, she could offer him landscaping work in her yard. The following summer Denver showed up at Nancy's door. At first she didn't remember him, but when a hawk flew through the yard as they talked, Denver said, "Look—there's a red-tailed hawk."

Denver recalls that Nancy asked, "How do you know it's a red-tailed hawk?"

"Because it has a red tail," he replied.

Nancy saw that Denver had a spark, perhaps some ambition. She put him to work landscaping her spacious property. A week later, when Denver again showed up for work, he noticed Nancy's Jeep was parked outside the garage, which was unusual. When he went to the door, Nancy said, "No landscaping today. We're going birding."

Brand-new Bushnell 7x35 binoculars, still in the box, were resting on the passenger seat when Denver went to get into the vehicle.

"That's for you," Nancy said, motioning to the binoculars.

Nancy perhaps saw Denver as a diamond in the rough, as someone in whom she could help develop and promote an interest in wildlife, encouraging him to pursue a career in the field of research.

Nancy schooled Denver in the habits of successful people. She taught him the importance of being organized, a habit that has followed him throughout his life. Nancy was also a model of positive persistence, another trait that defines Denver.

While an undergraduate student in wildlife biology at the University of Montana, Denver and a classmate published a scientific paper detailing observations of nesting northern pygmy owls and northern saw-whet owls. They spent many hours observing a snag where a pair of each of the owl species had nested, the pygmy owl nest in a cavity only a little way above the saw-whet owl's nest cavity—an unusual occurrence.

Denver had always been drawn to predatory mammals and raptors. Now owls were starting to exert their hold on the young student's imagination.

Denver threw himself into his studies, gaining proficiency

with statistics, population sampling, and methods of data collection and analysis—all skills a wildlife biologist needs.

His attention to detail also blossomed. As a punter on the University of Montana football team, Denver scribbled notes on his kicking shoe, instructing him how to angle his foot to send the football high and short, or low and long.

Denver picked up seasonal summer work with non-government conservation groups, observing, managing, and protecting nesting terns, gulls, and short-eared owls in Massachusetts.

He loved the fieldwork, roaming rich habitats and having frequent encounters with varied birds and mammals, gathering data much like a chipmunk gathers acorns for future consumption.

Biting insects and long days under a hot summer sun didn't deter Denver from his work. In his gut, he knew he didn't want to work indoors, feeling chained to a desk or a job for which he had no calling. Wildlife, and owls in particular, were becoming his passion.

After graduating with a bachelor's degree in wildlife biology, an idea began to percolate in his brain. Could he start his own nonprofit research group to study owls? Denver perused the wildlife literature and realized that no one seemed to be studying the western owls with long-term studies, unlike the crowded fields of grizzly bear, wolf, and mountain lion research. The riveting faces of owls drew Denver's attention. To him, these iconic birds were practically begging to be studied.

Denver knew that time pressures forced students to produce publishable research that often limited their fieldwork to one or two years. He also knew that meaningful wildlife data often comes only from multiyear or multidecade studies, which Denver reasoned could be his niche. He ran the idea past trusted friends and family.

Nancy Claflin kicked in seed money to help Denver start the Owl Research Institute. Nancy's friends Nan and Bill Harris later joined with their own contributions to Denver and ORI. Both Nancy and Nan have passed away, but their early support and direction lives on. Today the institute still operates on donations and grants. Denver credits Nancy with the gentle, supportive push that got him to where he is today. At ORI, a reading room and library are dedicated to her.

"[Nancy] took me under her wing when I was sixteen years old and gave me this world of birds," said Denver in a November 1998 story in the *Missoulian*, a newspaper, a year after he had bought a seven-acre farm in the Mission Valley and established a research and education center.

"Nancy gave me this so I could give it to others," said Denver.

Nowadays, Denver and ORI researchers spend many days a year in the field. He pays little heed to a few hardships like hiking long miles on snowshoes in deep Montana snow or needing to free an ATV deeply mired in tundra mud. Denver relishes the back-to-back days spent outside, watching and taking the measure of a most impressive study subject, the snowy owl. And that's just where he wants to be, doing what he envisioned all those years ago.

← Nancy Claflin holds an eastern screech-owl.

CHAPTER 3
WHO'S NESTING?

Sometime in early to mid-June Denver lands in Utqiagvik and he hits the ground running. He pulls his two all-terrain vehicles (ATVs) out of warehouse storage and fires them up to make sure they are operating smoothly. His big two-seater Polaris ATV will be his main transportation around town and to the outlands of his study area.

Snow, deeply drifted in places, still coats the tundra, though with twenty-four-hour daylight and above-freezing temperatures, it's starting to retreat from the land.

Denver also unpacks heavy parkas, hats, and mittens from storage. He will need these for riding the ATV in the raw, cold weather of summer in Utqiagvik. A fur-trimmed hood, neoprene face covering, and ski goggles will keep his head toasty.

Finding summer housing in Utqiagvik can be a scramble. Denver often subleases

← Early June on the tundra finds this melt hole in the snow where a female snowy owl has been incubating her five eggs.

an apartment from a schoolteacher who's away for the summer break. Denver prefers this to living in the dormitories run by the Ukpeagvik Inupiat Corporation (UIC), whose logo is a flying snowy owl. Visiting researchers and scientists end up staying in UIC dorms named Ukpik Nest I and Ukpik Nest II.

In 1992 Denver initiated the Snowy Owl Breeding Ecology and Lemming Population Study in Utqiagvik when it was called Barrow. He decided to base his study in a one-hundred-square-mile area of tundra and ponds that encompassed the town. In hindsight, Denver says, "I didn't realize how much work it would take to cover such a big area."

While Denver's research isn't funded by UIC, he maintains close ties to its many Inupiat employees, as they offer support in other ways. Perhaps it's directing him on how to access a remote area via a hunter's trail, or repairing a broken ATV, or providing a summer field assistant or two for his research, or supplying storage space for ATVs, equipment,

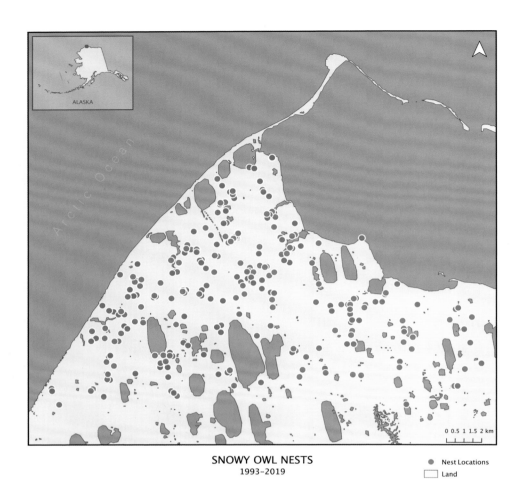

SNOWY OWL NESTS
1993–2019

● Nest Locations
☐ Land

↑ Red dots on this map show where Denver Holt has documented snowy owl nests from 1993 to 2020 in his study area.

← This female snowy owl returns to her nest to incubate her six eggs.

and reference books that he wants to leave in place, ready for the following field season.

Denver frequently visits the UIC labs to discuss research with scientists in other fields of inquiry. This cross-pollination of ideas keeps all the researchers on their toes and excited about their work.

While Denver makes it a point to socialize with other researchers in Utqiagvik, usually over friendly potluck suppers held in the dorms' large dining rooms, he prefers the ample space and quiet of a private apartment to stay organized and productive.

Denver quickly but methodically creates a field office in his apartment. He sets up at a six-foot-long (almost two-meter-long) folding plastic table to serve as his desk. It faces a window that looks out over pools of standing water in the side yard. Here a tiny shorebird called a red-necked phalarope swims, spinning and twirling as she pecks and dabs at tiny invertebrates. At the edge of the pool, a bright male black-and-white snow bunting flutters in to feed a gray chick who's just learning to fly. During summer in Utqiagvik, birds are never far away.

Above the table, on a wide window ledge, Denver sets out his library of reference books on birds, plants, insects, mammals, climate, statistics, and other topics of scientific interest. Spread across the table in organized fashion next to his laptop computer are many papers he is writing, editing, or reviewing for scientific journals.

Denver lays out more scientific papers in various stages of completion, lining them up along the wall on the carpeted floor beneath the table. Publishing papers in scientific journals from years of data Denver has collected and analyzed is what drives his summer work with snowy owls and all the other owl species he studies in Montana.

During some summer field seasons, Denver may need to move once or twice to new apartments. Being a scientist can impose a lifestyle that he endures but doesn't particularly enjoy. Denver has experience moving boxes of books and bulky furniture on an ATV. The owl researcher sometimes has to adopt the nomadic habits of his study subjects!

Once in town, Denver is anxious to get into the field to see if snowy owls are nesting in his hundred-square-mile study area. He will visit every corner of his plot at least twice, and often more times than that. For some visits, he drives onto a gravel road shoulder (there are no paved roads in Utqiagvik), parks his ATV, and then hikes onto the tundra.

Denver frequently stops to scan with his 10-power binoculars. Hike and scan. Hike and scan. Hike and scan. Denver may walk eight, ten, or twelve miles (twelve, sixteen, or nineteen kilometers) in this way, searching a large swath

← Denver sets up his field office in a different place every summer. Some summers he has to move his field office as he hustles for housing.

of tundra for the telltale white horizontal speck—a female snowy owl brooding eggs on the top of a mound, perhaps with another white vertical speck nearby—an attending male snowy owl.

But distant white specks might not always be snowy owls. Denver often stands atop a mound to gain the advantage of two or three feet (about one meter) of elevation. Wavy heat shimmers rise from the tundra and distort binocular views. Denver hikes great distances to close the gap on white specks to see if indeed they are brooding female snowy owls. Instead, the white speck might be a pale glaucous gull sitting on a nest, or a piece of plastic trash imitating a brooding snowy owl.

After decades of study, Denver knows that only the whitest, brightest male snowy owls get to nest. Not coincidentally, older snowy owls are whiter and brighter, with few or no markings on their feathers. Younger males have more markings on their plumage. Younger males may hang out on the tundra, scoping the scene, but they don't get to nest.

To get to the more remote parts of his study area, Denver drives his ATV onto the tundra, usually following trails left by caribou hunters traveling on ATVs or snow machines. These trails often cross big patches of soft, water-logged soil. Denver drives over these swampy places slowly, his 850-lb 4x4 ATV usually clawing its way through the mud.

One fine Arctic day in July, I rented an ATV so I could follow Denver as he headed out to check a far corner of the study site.

As Denver left the gravel road that leads south out of town, I saw his ATV lurch onto the tundra with a big splash.

"Wow," said Denver. "I don't think I've ever seen the tundra this wet."

With permafrost trapping rainwater on the surface, the tundra becomes a giant green and brown sponge with hidden deep pockets of water and muck that easily swallow an ATV.

Sometimes the mud wins and the big ATV gets stuck, mired in brown tundra goo. When that happens, it's all hands on deck as Denver pulls up his hip boots, steps off his machine into the chocolate pudding, and pushes the ATV, trying to rock it free from the sucking mud. If you happen to be the lucky passenger riding in the rear seat (on this day it was Hannah, a recent college graduate on her day off from a summer biologist job), you will be pressed into service to help push.

→ Denver and Hannah dig the big ATV out from its muddy mire.

↑ A male snow bunting forages on tundra that's sprouting a colorful display of flowers.

↑ Two snow bunting chicks, beaks agape, wait to be fed as they hunker in their insulating ground nest that's lined with caribou hair and white feathers, possibly from a snowy owl.

We tried to pull Denver's ATV out using mine, but then mine got stuck! We freed my ATV easily, as it was smaller and lighter, so while Hannah dug muck away from the wheels of Denver's beast, I drove around behind it. Denver attached a steel tow cable and I slowly pulled Denver's machine backwards out of the quagmire. High-fives all around. Once under way, we crossed boggy streams and stretches of land that looked more like a bayou than tundra.

For close-to-town areas of his study site, we glass the tundra from the road as we sit perched atop our parked ATVs. At a few spots, we climb onto the roof of an abandoned building or a gas well shed to use a tripod-mounted spotting scope to pull in distant details.

Some summers, snowy owls seem to be nesting all across the tundra, each nest a shallow scrape in the earth atop a grassy mound. Other summers, snowy owls don't nest anywhere in Denver's study area.

Denver, along with a handful of researchers at other Arctic sites, have long known that snowy owls need a plentiful supply of lemmings if they are going to nest.

Lemming populations fluctuate from year to year. During those summers when lemmings are scarce, male snowy owls hang around the tundra, likely occupying the nesting territory they would've used had there been more lemmings. The males look a bit lost, like warriors without a cause. During non-nesting summers, the female snowy owls seem to disperse. Denver doesn't know where they go. No one does, really. The remote vastness of the Arctic region and highly unpredictable bad weather make it difficult and expensive to visit other sites during a short summer research window. Few owl researchers are out there looking.

Denver never knows what each summer will bring, so he doesn't try to predict if the owls will nest in the coming year. He won't see who's nesting until he gets his boots on the tundra and starts searching.

In recent summers, one of Denver's first priorities upon arrival in Utqiagvik is setting up a solar-powered webcam to stream twenty-four-hour coverage of a nesting pair of snowy owls. (That live stream is carried online at www.explore.org.) To do that, Denver must first find an owl pair nesting fairly close, but not too close, to a road. That way, he and a work crew can wheel the heavy camera, batteries, and solar panels onto the wet tundra.

The crew quickly sets the camera up so they don't keep the female snowy owl off her eggs for much time.

The public finds the webcam's feed of the snowy owl nest fascinating, as evidenced by tens of thousands of views it gets. But for ORI, it's more than a social media sensation. The unblinking recording of activity at the nest from June to September creates a picture of owl behavior. Later, after the nesting season, Denver or another ORI researcher can analyze the video, drawing data from it.

How often does the female snowy owl leave the nest? Are humans walking on the tundra, causing the female to leave the nest? How often does the male deliver food? What does he bring? How often does the female sleep? When do the eggs hatch? Does the male ever incubate the eggs? How long does the male linger at the nest after delivering prey? These questions and so many more can be answered and quantified by studying archived webcam video of the nesting owls.

Since the snowy owl pair quickly accept the presence of the somewhat distant webcam, their behavior soon returns to normal. It's possible to observe their natural behavior via the footage, whereas a human observer at the same distance from the nest would cause a disturbance. Not to mention that a human in a blind wouldn't be able to observe for twenty-four

remote location is expensive and difficult. Denver notes that the hardware, transport, and installation of the snowy owl webcam costs tens of thousands of dollars, which luckily is paid for by Explore.org. Just transporting the hardware for the setup in Ukqiagvik means flying it in as air cargo or floating it in on the summer barge.

The camera runs off a solar panel charging a bank of heavy batteries, since it is miles from any electrical outlets. The setup needs to be weatherproof to operate in rain, snow, high wind, and twenty-four-hour sun or overcast skies.

In Montana, if the great gray owl nest that calls for a webcam happens to be forty-five feet (fourteen meters) up in a fir snag, setting a camera at eye level means someone has to climb an adjacent tree with the video camera and its power supply. This work must be carried out quickly so as not to disturb the nesting owl. Great gray owls often aggressively defend their nests from human intruders.

Engaging the public through a webcam at an owl nest increases support for ORI's research and generates goodwill for the owls. A webcam gives people who may never see snowy owls on their Arctic nesting grounds an intimate peek at fuzzy gray chicks and two good-looking, hard-working parents.

By the time I arrived in Utqiagvik in late June, Denver had found five active snowy owl nests. Shortly thereafter, the male snowy owl from one of the nests most distant from town turned up dead. His mate, who had been incubating seven eggs, would now be forced to leave the nest to hunt.

Left unattended, the eggs would be exposed to the cold and predators such as arctic foxes, glaucous gulls, and pomarine jaegers. Predators quickly take note of an exposed unattended nest of big white owl eggs. With the death of the

hours a day, seven days a week.

Conversely, a webcam can't supply certain quantitative data: What does a chick weigh? How often is the male tangling off-camera with pomarine jaegers? How many eggs are in the nest? What prey species have been dropped off by the male? Was that a brown lemming or a collared lemming the male just delivered? That's where a personal inspection of the nest by Denver comes into play.

Meanwhile, back at the ORI office in Charlo, Montana, Liberty DeGrandpre, who wears many hats in the office, monitors and moderates the webcam comments that flow in response to the riveting video of the snowy owls' nest life. Later in the summer Liberty twice flew up to Utqiagvik to assist Denver with lemming surveys and owl chick banding.

Why aren't webcams used more? Setting a webcam up at a

← Denver stops and scans to watch a distant pair of nesting snowy owls.

male, the female's chances of raising a family of fuzzy owl chicks had suddenly turned to zero.

Denver collected the corpse of the brilliant white male. There were no signs the owl had been shot. In fact, the male seemed to be in perfect condition other than the fact he was dead. As of publication time, Denver was still waiting for a veterinarian to perform a necropsy to determine what killed him. Luckily, Denver doesn't often find dead owls in his research area.

The four other snowy owl nests that Denver had located all had eggs or newly hatched chicks, four or five per nest.

This would be a moderate year on the tundra for breeding snowy owls but by no means a banner year. In the summer of 1995 Denver logged fifty-six snowy owl nests in his study area, the most he's ever recorded.

During the summers of 1994, 1997, 1998, 2001, 2004, 2007, 2009, 2010, 2013, 2017, and 2020, no snowy owls nested in Denver's study area. Not coincidentally, brown lemmings were scarce those same summers.

SEXING AN OWL FROM THE 4TH SECONDARY FEATHER

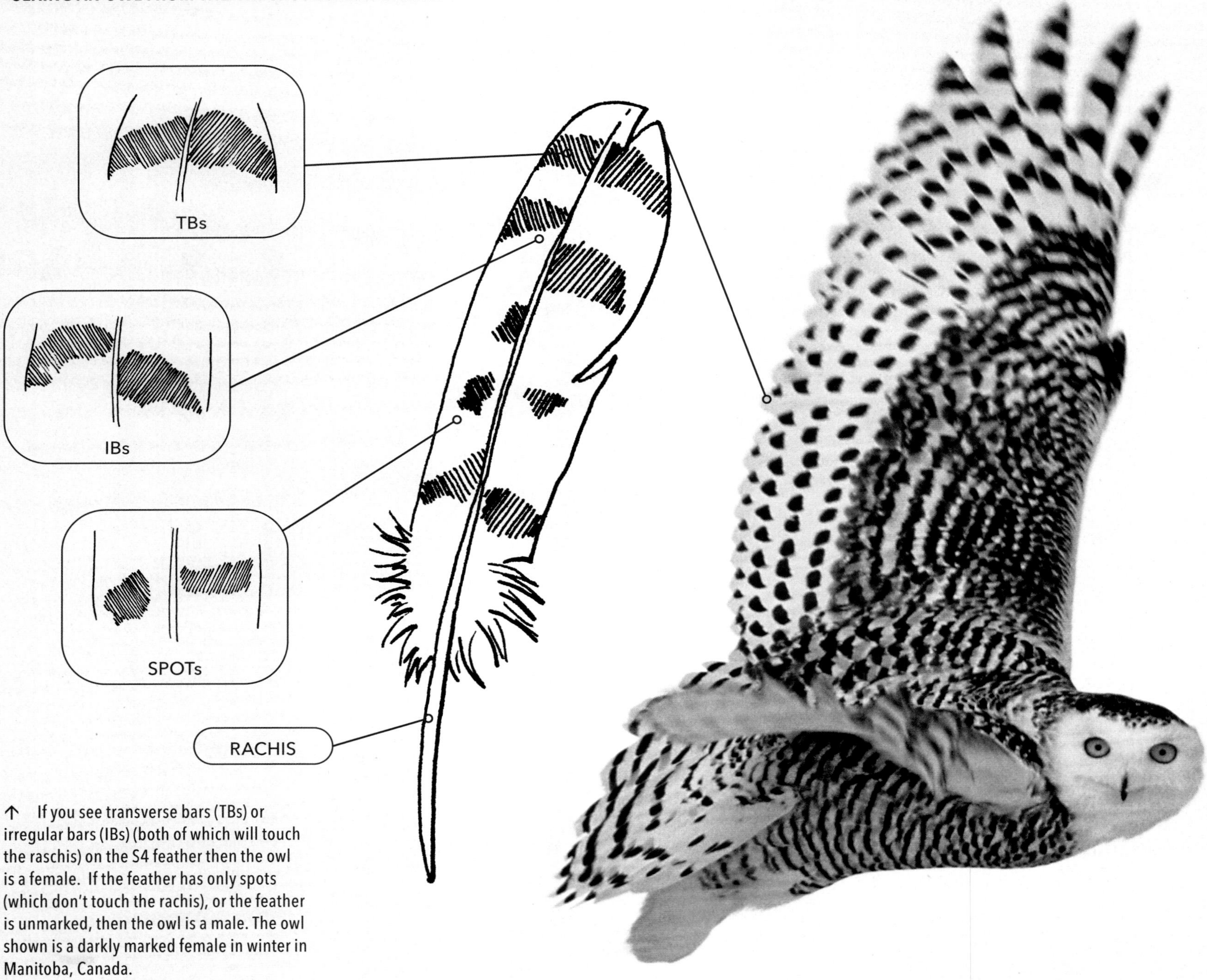

TBs

IBs

SPOTs

RACHIS

↑ If you see transverse bars (TBs) or irregular bars (IBs) (both of which will touch the raschis) on the S4 feather then the owl is a female. If the feather has only spots (which don't touch the rachis), or the feather is unmarked, then the owl is a male. The owl shown is a darkly marked female in winter in Manitoba, Canada.

Female or Male?

Migrating young owls have darker markings than their parents. Females are the darkest, with heavy bars marching down their chests, bellies, backs, and upper wings. A young male snowy owl will wear darker markings than its brilliant white father and may look awfully similar to its mother.

Denver always notes the markings on every snowy owl he observes. On the tundra, he would often exclaim, "Look how white that male is. He absolutely glows!" or he would advise, "Watch that female on the nest. She'll get darker markings after she molts and grows new feathers."

Determining gender can be a tricky business with young males looking similar to females. Denver and other ORI researchers developed a near foolproof way to tell the young males apart from females. The catch is that you'll need to get a good look at a single particular feather in the owl's wing. And that's easier said than done.

One way to glimpse that particular feather is to wait for the owl to fly and then snap a series of high-speed photos that freeze or stop the movement of the owl's wings. Then you can study the wing photos at your leisure, paying close attention to S4, the fourth secondary feather in the wing.

But first, a feather geography lesson is in order.

Starting from the outermost tip of the wing, wend your way toward the back edge of the wing, counting those big finger-like feathers as you go. These are primary feathers. There are ten on each wing.

Continuing down the rear edge of the wing, you'll next encounter the secondary feathers. Count down to the fourth one. Bingo! That is the one you'll need to study carefully. That's the one Denver says will reveal the sex of the young owl.

↑ A molted snowy owl wing feather rests alongside cotton grass on the tundra.

↑ Denver studies a molted primary feather likely from a non-breeding male snowy owl.

← Dark markings show that this is a young female who probably hatched the previous summer in the Arctic. This bird was photographed during winter in Manitoba, Canada.

FEMALE WING

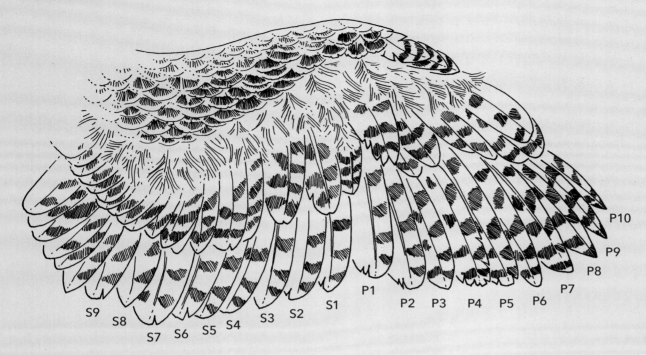

S9 S8 S7 S6 S5 S4 S3 S2 S1 P1 P2 P3 P4 P5 P6 P7 P8 P9 P10

← The back edge of the snowy owl wing has two types of feathers, called primary (P) and secondary (S) feathers. Look to the S4 to see what types of markings show. Female owls will have transverse bars or irregular bars on the S4 that touch the feather shaft (also called the rachis).

→ At right, a female snowy owl's splayed wing reveals the S4 feather, which is most easily viewed on a flying bird.

MALE WING

→ Male snowy owls have spots or no markings on the S4 feather. Spots do not touch the rachis of the S4 feather.

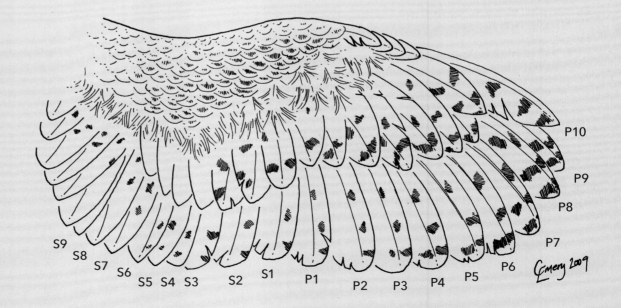

S9 S8 S7 S6 S5 S4 S3 S2 S1 P1 P2 P3 P4 P5 P6 P7 P8 P9 P10

Emery 2009

How did Denver and his team figure all this out? They photographed the secondary and primary feather patterns of 140 older snowy owl chicks and drew blood from each bird to run a DNA test to determine each one's sex.

Denver's team described three types of dark markings on secondary feathers: transverse bars, irregular bars, and spots. The team predicted that males would have few or no bars and more spots on the secondary feathers, while females would have few to no spots but more bars on the secondary feathers. The researchers carefully studied markings on the wing feathers, trying to correlate certain markings with the bird's sex. Eventually they zeroed in on the S4 feather markings.

If S4 spots don't touch the feather shaft (called the rachis), or if spots are absent, you are looking at a male. If bars touch the rachis of S4, you are looking at a female.

They found that their prediction of who is a male and who is a female based on S4 markings was exactly right when checked against the blood DNA test.

And that's an impressive example of biological detective work pulled off in a harsh environment!

CHAPTER 4
COUNTING AVINNAQ

One day in early July, Denver and I, both encased in hip-high rubber boots, squish across an expanse of tundra, threading our way between earthen mounds thrust upward by subterranean ice wedges. Denver points out the rough polygonal shape of the large mounds. Some of them are riddled with muddy runways, tunnels through the grass, and holes in the soil.

I follow Denver closely as we angle toward a distant mound topped by a thin upright stick—a marker for the start of a lemming sampling transect.

To count lemmings, Denver lays out three randomly placed line transects in separate parts of his study area. Each transect is just over half a mile (one kilometer) long. Roughly every ninety-eight feet (thirty meters), Denver sets ten snap traps inside a circle thirty-two feet (ten meters) in diameter, for a total of one hundred traps per transect. Denver checks the traps for dead lemmings daily over the course

← Studying breeding snowy owls also means studying brown lemmings.

of three or five days. This means walking miles (kilometers), slogging across squishy tundra.

"Avinnaq," Denver suddenly blurts, peering down at the tundra. I'm not even sure what Denver has just said, but he sounds excited and certainly emphatic.

I look to where he's peering. I barely catch a glimpse of a dark brown streak running along a muddy runway, tunneling through the grass. I've just seen a snowy owl's summer diet must-have: a brown lemming.

The brown streak disappears into a hole in a mound of turf. Denver looks pleased. He usually does when he sees lemmings. He tells me that *avinnaq* is the Inupiat word for lemming.

We inspect the hole the lemming just dove into. Piles of football-shaped turds decorate the entrance. Lemmings defecate a lot. In fact, a researcher from the University of Texas who was working in Utqiagvik later tells me that brown lemmings drop their body weight in poop—every

↑ A collared lemming sits atop a pile of owl pellets in a scientist's gloved hand. The pellets are full of the fur and bones of other lemmings, but don't tell the lemming!

← If you are a carnivore and you live in the Arctic, the chances are good you eat brown lemmings.

twenty-four hours! That means a lemming would have to eat more than its body weight in plant matter every day.

With all that lemming manure getting dropped on and around mounds, it's no surprise that plants seem to grow better there. The mounds resemble little tundra hotbeds of plant extravagance—more flowers, lusher grass, more insects, all of which attracts more birds.

Many more times during our tundra hike, Denver exclaims, *"Avinnaq!"* Soon I too am flushing lemmings with each footfall. The fleet-footed rodents look like dark little hamsters. They dodge footsteps and zip, dashing down their matted, muddy runways. Their lives depend on speed and their ability to find cover in the blink of an eye. Catch one in your gloved hand if you dare. Lemmings nip, but perhaps lemmings will charm you. Not as beady-eyed as a deer mouse and not as jarringly big or alarming as a rat, lemmings live by their wits, as these plump rascals drive the food chain for many birds and mammals.

If you are a carnivore and you live in the Arctic tundra, you likely eat lemmings. For lemmings, death usually comes from above—the snapping jaws of a pouncing arctic fox, the grabbing talons of a snowy owl, the razor-sharp hooked beak of a pomarine jaeger, flinging aside turf as it digs for the nervous lemming.

Two species of lemmings inhabit the tundra of Denver's study area. Brown lemmings live on wet tundra and are the most abundant. Collared lemmings inhabit dryer tundra and are less common. Brown lemmings constitute 90 percent or more of a snowy owl's diet in the summer, as Denver has

↑ A grass-eye view of a brown lemming might look like this. This rodent feeds on grasses and sedges.

↑ Collared lemmings live on drier tundra than brown lemmings.

determined by dissecting and analyzing some 35,000 snowy owl pellets. Pellets are the indigestible, regurgitated feathers, hair, and bone castings from an owl's previous meal.

Dissecting thousands of pellets won't reveal every animal a snowy owl has eaten, but pellet contents are useful for determining the bulk of an owl's diet. Denver has found remains of thirty-three species of mammals and birds in snowy owl pellets. But he's noted thirty-six prey species left on the rim of snowy owl nests. If the owl consumes only meat but no feathers, fur, or bones, a pellet won't contain evidence of that meal, or that species of animal.

The diets of the two lemming species differ in important ways. Brown lemmings munch monocots—namely grasses and sedges. Guess where grasses and sedges prevail? Wet tundra. That's where you'll find brown lemmings.

Collared lemmings dine on dicots—flowering plants such as louseworts, arctic willow, saxifrages, and other colorful flowering plants. Where do dicots flourish? Dry tundra. That's where collared lemmings live.

As lemmings go, so go snowy owls. Nesting success for snowy owls relies on abundant brown lemmings more than anything else. Denver has been sampling lemming populations since the beginning of his snowy owl study in Utqiagvik. His data shows an unmistakable link between lemming abundance and how many owl chicks a snowy owl pair will fledge.

In years when lemmings are abundant, a female owl may lay up to eight eggs. During a summer when lemmings are present in low to moderate numbers, female owls lay only three to five eggs. In summers when lemmings are scarce, no eggs are laid.

→ Liberty and Denver walk to one of three lemming transects. Note the abundant cotton grass underfoot.

"Not everybody's doing this," says Denver, breaking into a grin as we slog a transect, periodically stooping to check traps. Raindrops patter off our parkas and a cold wind cuts out of the east, fresh off the Arctic Ocean. Denver considers this just another day at the "office."

He weighs each trapped lemming, then sexes each one before popping it into a labeled plastic bag, which goes into his backpack. He records this information in a field notebook. Denver will dissect female lemmings later to determine if they are pregnant. Ultimately he is trying to figure out whether or not female lemmings have larger litters during years when lemmings are abundant, and whether

or not they have smaller or no litters during years when lemmings are scarce.

The work can seem tedious. Denver often works with an assistant, which makes the chore of walking transects more interesting and maybe even fun.

Over the years Denver has employed local Inupiat as field research assistants. Some summers, a researcher from ORI will fly in to assist Denver. One recent summer, Denver had field research assistance from Liberty DeGrandpre. She wanted to come to Utqiagvik to see how Denver studied snowy owls and lemmings.

Liberty joined Denver, taking a break from her regular job

↑ Denver records weights as Liberty weighs each lemming they caught.

↑ Dressed for a chilly commute, Liberty and Denver (driving) head out to check a lemming sampling transect.

of running the ORI office, website, social media, promotion, and fundraising. She wanted a taste of tundra walking, searching for snowy owl nests and chicks, and counting lemmings.

Since the beginning of his lemming surveys, Denver checks his traplines daily for five days. In summer he conducts three trapping sessions—one each in June, July, and August. That means he'll be trekking over miles of tundra for three days of trap setting and fifteen days of trap checking. Eighteen days of tundra walking means you will be rained on, probably sleeted on, and likely snowed on. You definitely will be buffeted by cutting winds.

Once you spend time on the tundra, you learn to pay attention to the wind and its direction. A west wind brings wet. An east wind or a north wind brings cold. A south wind brings warmth and mosquitoes. Denver notes that the

mosquitoes are rarely horrendous, though he does travel with a head net in his daypack.

As Liberty would later write in an email to me, slogging across wet tundra to check traps was "somewhat miserable at times" but she was glad she made the trip. "Those kind of experiences make the best memories!" she wrote. "Such a very special time in my life for sure!"

The summer I visited Denver he decided to shorten his lemming sampling runs to three days. He felt the data would still be valid from three three-day trapping sessions in place of three five-day trapping sessions. I think Denver was privately relieved to have fewer tundra schleps to contend with. Liberty and I? We certainly didn't miss those extra six days of multimile tundra walking.

Navigating across squishy *nuna* (the Inupiaq word for "land" and "tundra") in bulky hip boots means burning

→ Steller's eider drakes cruise a tundra pond.

lots of calories. (Imagine walking across a giant open-face fluffernutter sandwich and you'll have a rough idea of what wet tundra walking entails.) At the end of each snowy owl field season, Denver returns to Montana a lesser man—literally. He will have lost ten or more pounds from his rigorous fieldwork.

By my third week in Utqiagvik, I noticed my pants were loose on my waist. I too was losing weight from miles of walking and strenuous ATV driving. Plus, just to stay warm and energized, I emulated Denver, shoveling handfuls of gorp (a snack of mixed nuts and dried fruit) and strips of dried mango and salmon jerky into my mouth as I trudged the wet land.

After years of gathering lemming data, Denver has come to the surprising conclusion that lemming populations, at least in Utqiagvik, don't follow a regular cycle or pattern of highs and lows. Many researchers working in other regions of the Arctic suggest that lemming populations are cyclic, they rise and fall over a two-, three-, or four-year cycle.

In ORI's annual newsletter, the *Roost,* Denver notes: "Our data does not support the theory of lemming cycles: the interval between peaks is highly variable and the

amplitude and density are never the same from year to year."

Simply stated, the lemming population dips and peaks randomly, at least in Denver's study area.

So then, the mystery remains: How do snowy owls decide if they will nest? How do snowy owls manage to arrive at locations where lemming numbers are high? The Arctic is vast, and much of the region supports few if any lemmings. Denver has yet to see a snowy owl taking notes from one of his lemming sampling transects. Somehow, the owls gauge the lemming population and lay or don't lay eggs in accordance with it.

Up until a couple of years ago, the U.S. Fish and Wildlife Service trapped arctic foxes in Denver's study area in an effort to decrease predation on eggs and ducklings of Steller's eiders, a federally listed endangered species. Denver believes, though he can't yet prove it with data, that the trapping of foxes has caused lemming numbers to decline.

Perhaps connected to that decline, Denver has seen a slow decline in the snowy owl numbers nesting around Utqiagvik.

"When foxes are around everything seems to do better. We see more lemmings. On a high lemming year, we see more Lapland longspurs," says Denver.

More foxes keep plant-grazing geese in check. This means there's more plants for the lemmings to eat.

"What drives it all? Figuring that out is the hard part," says Denver. "[A big lemming year] only happens once in a while—it's kind of like a bumper crop year where so many factors come together."

And when those bumper crop years occur with lemmings, Denver finds snowy owls nesting all across his tundra study area.

Lemmings of Urban Legend

If you, like a surprising number of people, believe that the tundra spawns waves of lemmings that leap off cliffs and into the sea, think again. You have been fooled by an urban legend that probably originated with fabricated scenes of unrealistic lemming behavior in the 1958 Walt Disney movie *White Wilderness,* a film in the studio's True Life Adventure series.

Filmed in Alberta, Canada (which has no ocean shoreline), the movie shows scores of lemmings supposedly leaping into the Arctic Ocean, driven by a great migratory urge. The lemmings in the film were actually imported from Churchill, Manitoba.

How do I know this? In 1994, my wife, Marcia, and I were honeymooning in Churchill, a birdwatching mecca. I happened to strike up a conversation with a resident of the town and somehow our talk turned to lemmings. He told me that when he was a kid, people connected to the movie came to town and offered to buy all the lemmings the local kids could catch. If I recall correctly, he said he was paid twenty-five cents per lemming.

The captured brown lemmings were transported nearly a thousand miles (1,609 kilometers) to the film set in Calgary, according to a Canadian Broadcasting Corporation television program called *Cruel Camera,* a show that revealed some of the cruelties and abuses to which animals in Hollywood movies have been exposed to create gripping, impactful action footage.

I quote a Wikipedia post about the film: "Bob McKeown, the host of the CBC program, discovered that the lemming scene was filmed at the Bow River near downtown Calgary, and not in the Arctic Ocean as implied by the film. McKeown interviewed a lemming expert, who claimed that the particular species of lemming shown in the film is not known

↑ Widespread misperceptions of lemmings are likely attributable to staged scenes in a popular 1950s film. The lemming depicted in this photo is behaving normally.

to migrate, much less commit mass suicide. Additionally, he revealed that footage of a polar bear cub falling down an Arctic ice slope was really filmed in a Calgary film studio."

Various other published stories report that the film crew threw lemmings off the bank of the river, making it look like the rodents were leaping to their deaths by drowning in the Arctic Ocean.

Wildlife films are notorious for staging action or surprising situations to increase viewership. Wildlife scientists observe and document what really happens in the wild. Rest assured that Denver has never observed a mass of brown lemmings headed over a cliff, plunging into the sea.

CHAPTER 5
CHECKING ON CHICKS

During summer, the tundra around Utqiagvik is crawling with scientists and researchers from around the world. Mammologists, ornithologists, climatologists, botanists, ecologists, entomologists, waterfowl and shorebird biologists, meteorologists, geologists, cartographers, permafrost scientists, aerial imaging engineers, limnologists, and wildlife photographers poke, prod, walk on, fly over, spy on, measure, photograph, and talk about the tundra and the creatures that live there. And that's just the visitors.

Utqiagvik residents take to the land to hunt, fish, camp, gather berries, or just explore their big thawing backyard. At times, the tundra can seem a bit crowded. Thankfully, hunters and fishers tend to stick to established trails in their quest for game. Perhaps it's the occasional cross-country, off-trail sightseer on an ATV that presents the greatest potential disturbance to a nesting snowy owl.

Luckily, many of the visiting researchers

← From afar, Liberty and Denver study a snowy owl nest, trying to locate chicks.

conduct their studies within view of a gravel road. Only the shorebird and waterfowl biologists and Denver wander farther afield. So, despite the seasonal influx of researchers, the snowy owls have large tracts of tundra that see few or brief periods of human activity.

Snowy owls notice all that moves in their immediate surroundings. Female owls incubating eggs on the nest have a sweeping view of the tundra around them since the nest is always situated atop a grassy mound. The female watches where her mate is hunting for lemmings, and she will let him know when she and the chicks are hungry by giving a shrill call, demanding food.

"Snowy owls are different from other birds," says Denver. "The female's first line of defense is leaving the nest at any sign of a human. Snowy owls are different, except for maybe sandhill cranes."

Most Arctic-nesting birds are slow to leave the nest even when humans are nearby. In contrast, a nesting female snowy

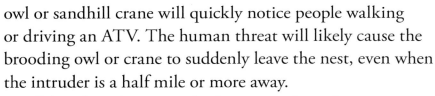
↑ A mother snowy owl and her chicks glow under the midnight sun. The male has brought in lemmings for them to eat (visible at left and right).

↑ Five snowy owl chicks watch a distant parent, waiting for the arrival of food.

owl or sandhill crane will quickly notice people walking or driving an ATV. The human threat will likely cause the brooding owl or crane to suddenly leave the nest, even when the intruder is a half mile or more away.

If that disturbance is a biologist searching for nesting shorebirds or a wildlife photographer trying for spectacled eider photos, the person may not realize they caused the mother owl to leave her nest, potentially keeping a female off her eggs or chicks for an hour or more.

If the air is cold or rain is falling and wind is blowing, uncovered eggs rapidly chill. The exposed eggs become vulnerable to aerial predators like ravens, jaegers, and glaucous gulls or ground predators like arctic foxes, all of which are less wary of humans than a nesting snowy owl. The eggs are in real danger. The nest may fail.

Once the person leaves the area, the female snowy owl quickly returns to the nest. The male returns to sentry duty or, if there are hungry chicks in the nest, he continues to hunt.

To gather data on snowy owls, Denver tries to visit each nest every four to five days. He admits that each visit is a stressor for the owls. However, Denver is careful to minimize that stress. He never visits nests on rainy days or when it's cold, or if the winds are high. His short visits minimize the time the female is off the nest.

As he approaches a nest from afar, Denver's eyes are glued to the sitting female—a horizontal white speck on top of a mound.

Once the female flushes from the nest, the second line of defense comes when the male flies toward Denver, circling and uttering deep alarm barks. As Denver goes to the nest,

The male snowy owl has just brought in a pectoral sandpiper chick for his hungry chicks. He will "beak" it off to his mate, who seems preoccupied with the chicks down in the nest.

the female may stand off at a distance, her deep alarm hoots sounding like barks.

The male owl often lands nearby, all the while glaring and woofing at the researcher. Often the male will bark a guttural *heck-heck-heck*. Particularly aggressive males will quickly fly toward Denver, making a direct pass at him. If he fails to duck, the male will strike, raking his talons across Denver's scalp or backpack. Denver has had more than one Gore-Tex jacket shredded by male snowy owls striking him as he measured eggs or weighed chicks in the nest.

He limits the time he spends at each nest to a few minutes so an incubating female can quickly get back to her eggs to warm them and protect them from prying predator eyes. Denver also monitors the movements and activities of other people working in the vicinity of nesting snowy owls. He's not shy about educating other researchers and the public about the special needs of nesting snowy owls and how a human presence can cause nest failure.

Denver weighs any prey that he finds at the nest. Most often the prey animals are brown lemmings, though the menu for nesting snowy owls lists thirty-six entrées of birds and mammals. An interesting finding is that lemmings weighed at the nest are nearly always heavier than the lemmings Denver catches on his sampling transects. Denver wonders if male snowy owls are consciously hunting larger lemmings as prey, or if there's some other factor in play.

When a snowy owl egg hatches after thirty to thirty-two days of incubation by the female, the tiny chick must hammer its way out of the egg using a little whitish bump on its beak known as an egg tooth.

Once out of the egg, the chick is blind, feeble, and unable to regulate its body temperature. The female owl keeps the tiny chick under her, warm and secure from a harsh environment. Only she will feed the chick when it is small. The female will tear morsels of meat from a lemming and gently offer the meat to the chick.

A snowy owl's clutch of eggs won't hatch all at once. The female incubates each egg as soon as it's laid. Since the female owl lays an egg every one to three days, the first egg laid will have a head start on development over the second egg. Egg number one will have a four- to six-day lead over the third egg.

In a big egg year, the first egg may hatch two weeks ahead of the last egg, which means there will be a large size difference between the oldest and youngest chicks. This method of egg laying and incubation results in asynchronous hatching, an adaptation found in many raptors.

Denver thinks that the staggered egg hatching helps ensure that at least some older chicks survive if prey becomes scarce during the nesting season. The oldest and biggest chicks in a nest might outcompete their smaller siblings by grabbing most of the food the female offers. In rare instances, the youngest chick may starve to death and its oldest sibling might eat it. It sounds brutal, but in those cases the oldest chicks get bigger and stronger and have an even better chance of survival.

Usually though, the mother owl is careful to feed all of her babies, including the smallest. When lemmings are abundant, there'll be ample food for all the chicks, and even the youngest ones have a decent chance at fledging.

→ While checking on chicks at the webcam nest, Denver hugs the ground, facedown, as the male snowy owl defends his chicks by striking Denver's pack with his talons.

↑ Snowy owl chicks huddle at the nest with their mother for protection and warmth. Meanwhile, the mother looks away, tracking the male's whereabouts as he hunts. Note the large size difference between the smallest chick and the largest chick towering over it.

Snowy Owl Quick Facts

Scientific name: *Bubo scandiacus*

Former scientific name: *Nyctea scandiaca*

Closest relative: Great horned owl, *Bubo virginianus*

World population: Data incomplete; no accurate numbers available.

Sexual dimorphism: Females are larger than males.

Weight: Female: 2–6.5 lbs.
Male: 1.5–5.5 lbs.

Body length: Female: 22–26 in.
Male: 21–23 in.

Wingspan: Female: 4 ft. 9 in.–6 ft.
Male: 3 ft. 10 in.–5 ft. 5in.

Flight speed: Likely capable of 50 mph or faster; though rarely observed, snowy owls can soar in flight.

Clutch size: 4–11 eggs, though there are records of 15 or 16 eggs in one nest.

Incubation: 31–33 days

Age of chicks when they leave the nest: 21 days on average

Age of chicks capable of sustained flight: 45–60 days

How far can an owl rotate its head? More than 200 degrees in each direction but not as far as 270 degrees, as many books claim. An owl's fourteen neck bones enable great head-turning ability.

Oldest recorded snowy owl in the wild: 24 years old: from a snowy owl banded at Boston's Logan Airport by Norman Smith in 1992. Twenty-three years after it was banded, it reappeared at the same airport and was retrapped by Smith. Multiple published reports mistakenly state the owl was recaptured in Montana.

Do snowy owls have long-term mates? Most likely not, since they are nomadic and nest in distantly separated locations from year to year.

← Captive snowy owls at a zoo—male (l) and female (r).

CHAPTER 6
PHOTOGRAPH QUIETLY, USE A LONG LENS

Having the privilege of photographing a pair of snowy owls at their tundra nest presents difficult challenges and big responsibilities. As a wildlife photojournalist, my first priority is the safety of the owls: adults, eggs, and chicks.

In a harsh environment like the Arctic, the line between successful nesting and nest failure is a thin one. A half hour of improper human behavior near nesting snowy owls can cause that nest to fail. Denver acts as a gatekeeper for access to snowy owls nesting around Utqiaġvik. Only a very few wildlife photographers get the nod to work with them in Denver's study area.

Denver set high standards for me to meet as I developed plans to photograph at an owl nest in his research area. And that is as it should be. The owls' welfare would come first. Poor weather could easily scuttle my plans.

Before my arrival in late June, Denver had scoped out a handsome pair of owls whose nest could be accessed with an easy half-mile hike from a gravel road. The nest was atop a mound in a low-key spot that would not be visible from a road or house, and the nest looked out over a beautiful setting of pristine tundra, clear of human clutter (buildings, satellite dishes, power lines, gas pipelines, dead vehicles, trash, etc.). A clean background would make for better photos.

My plan was to set up a photo blind (or "hide" as it is sometimes called) a good distance from the nest and use that as a base to safely observe and photograph the nest life of the owl family. Using a blind would enable me to stay out of sight

← A mother snowy owl broods her clan, with only one of her chicks visible as it safely snoozes under her protective gaze. Only by using a blind to hide in was I able to capture this tender scene.

My photo blind sits at far left. The white specks at far right are a female snowy owl on the nest with a male snowy owl flying towards her to deliver a lemming. Can you find the white speck that is another male snowy owl? He's a little more than a third of the way from the right edge of the photo and farther out on the tundra.

of the wary snowy owl parents as they met the demands of raising their chicks.

With me hidden from view, their behavior would be natural and relaxed. In addition, the blind would shelter me and my cameras from blasting wind and frequent rain showers.

Last, the blind would hide me from people who might be walking on the tundra. Denver and I didn't want to draw attention to the location of a nest or my blind, so staying hidden was important. While nonresidents and non-Natives of Utqiagvik need to secure a permit from UIC before they venture onto Inupiat land, Native residents travel the land at will.

Harsh, unpredictable Arctic weather was the wildcard that Denver and I dealt with daily. In anticipation of extended periods of bad weather, when I might not even pick up a camera or venture onto the tundra for several days or weeks running, I had scheduled a five-week stay in Utqiagvik. I hoped my visit would be lengthy enough to yield a week of good weather.

Wildlife photography that's squeezed by a short stay often influences the photographer to work in bad weather, which in turn might have fatal consequences for a nest of snowy owl eggs or chicks.

High winds and cold temperatures along with sporadic rainfall kept me from setting up my blind for several days. I knew the initial setup would cause the female snowy owl to flush from the nest for a short period of time. We would have to wait for a mild, dry day so eggs and chicks wouldn't get chilled.

I sat tight and read a lot in my dormitory room in Ukpik Nest I. Then I visited the cultural center museum in town and watched some movies at Denver's apartment. I slept a lot. Time slowed down.

And then the female snowy owl threw us a curve. On a calm, warm day, we had approached the nest from afar, intending to set up the blind, when Denver noticed something unusual. The female owl walked off the nest when she saw us approach, but she didn't fly off as Denver expected she would.

"I don't think she can fly," said Denver, studying her through binoculars as we stood several hundred yards (meters) away. Denver nixed the day's plan to set the blind.

"We can't go in to set up the blind until she can fly," he said. We were back to the waiting game, a common occurrence for wildlife photography in the Arctic.

For the next four days the mother snowy owl stayed grounded. A heavy molt in her primary feathers was keeping her from the air. Gaps in her wing feathers showed where some of her big flight feathers had dropped. She couldn't get enough lift because of the missing primary and secondary feathers, so she could only stand by her nest or run off a short distance if people approached.

Feathers are amazing when one thinks about what they do—protecting a bird from rain, snow, and wind, insulating a bird from cold, keeping sun off the bird's skin, and best of all, enabling a bird to fly. By the time summer rolls around, a bird's feathers are frayed, worn, and possibly dirty. Some feathers may have broken. It's time to drop (molt) those old feathers and grow knew ones. But birds don't molt their feathers all at once. That's why you don't see naked birds walking around.

We didn't want to risk having her walk away from the eggs or young chicks for a long period of time. This was only the second or third time in twenty-eight years of snowy owl research that Denver had seen a nesting female unable to fly because of a heavy molt. "Give her five or six days and we'll check on her again to see if she can fly," said Denver.

When another mild, calm day finally came, Denver and I parked our vehicles off the roadbed and set off on foot. I carried my folded blind slung over my shoulder, along with a big bag of long steel tent stakes and a hammer.

As we approached the nest territory, as if on cue the female flew from the nest and the brilliant white male angled toward us, barking alarms. We soon reached the nest that now had five gray fuzzy chicks, all hunkered in their shallow nest depression atop a grassy tundra mound.

Denver stood next to the nest and began striding away from it, counting his steps as he went. When he had paced off 165 feet (50 meters), he stopped.

"Okay, you can put the blind here," he said, looking down at the toe of his rubber boot. I quickly unfurled my tent blind and unrolled four guy lines, anchoring each with a long stake. Then I secured the interior wire metal frames of the blind with many more stakes, hammering them easily into the soft upper three inches (eight centimeters) of soil until I struck frozen earth four inches (ten centimeters) down: permafrost. Hammering the stakes into the icy soil was like driving spikes into concrete.

My army of tent stakes driven into permafrost would be my best friends, anchoring the blind for the days ahead when winds would whip at more than forty miles (sixty-four kilometers) per hour. A windblown blind that tore loose from its moorings could tumble and roll into the owl nest—a potential catastrophe. My multi-staked blind would need to stay put despite the Arctic gales.

In the few minutes it took me to set up the blind, Denver had hung back at the nest, examining the five chicks, checking on their health and development. One of the chicks seemed too small. Denver worried that it wasn't developing properly. The chick's four siblings were all much larger. They towered over the tiny chick. Days later, Denver and I found the chick's body a hundred feet (thirty meters) from the nest after more than thirty-six hours of rainy, cold, windy weather. The youngster probably succumbed to hypothermia after getting soaked in the rain—a tough reality on the Alaskan tundra and always a sad discovery for scientists like Denver who work there.

Denver and I left, walking away from the blind and owl nest territory. Once we had put several hundred yards (meters) between us and the nest, we turned and watched through binoculars, making sure the female owl promptly returned to the nest to warm her chicks.

She paid little attention to the new blind on her horizon. She had accepted it. The blind was ready for me to use, but that would come on another day.

A majority of wildlife photographers don't use blinds, sometimes because they don't know about them or sometimes because they don't want to go the expense and considerable work that a photo blind entails. For a hide to work effectively, the photographer must have assistance from another person.

To get into the shelter, both my assistant and I must come to it at the same time. And then, crucially, we both duck into it, disappearing from the owls' view for a minute or two. Be assured that both of the adult snowy owls will be watching intently from a distance. Then, after I get settled, my assistant exits, buttons up the door, and walks away, leaving me hidden inside. Since owls can't count, they think the humans have left the area.

49

↑ The father snowy owl (left) offers a lemming to the mother as the oldest chick looks on with great interest. Within seconds of the handoff, the male flies off to resume hunting. Note the differences in the plumage of the male and female snowy owl parents.

At the owl nest where I worked, the female owl would be back on the nest within fifteen minutes of my assistant leaving the blind.

After I put in eight or more hours observing and photographing, it's time to leave. It's best for the owls if I don't suddenly pop out of my hiding place, as this would startle them, perhaps causing them to mistrust the structure. Having an assistant walk out to the blind, duck into it for a moment, and then leave with me in tow is critical. Very soon, the mother owl is back on the nest.

On my most recent Arctic trip, I was lucky to have Liberty assisting me by walking me into and out of my blind.

During the course of three weeks I worked in my camouflaged hide when the weather allowed. It became my field office, and like Denver, I had places for things.

A highly useful piece of "office" furniture was a folding camp chair with a padded back. It might sound like a small detail, but having a backrest on the chair is important. When working within a small space, muscles quickly grow cold and start to cramp. Being able to slightly recline and stretch one's back is key to staying comfortable.

I also piled on the warm clothes. If I'm not comfortable,

↑ This snowy owl male took a break from hunting for his family—he just had a bath.

I won't be sharply focused on watching the snowy owls. Capturing fleeting moments on camera takes patience and unwavering focus. I find it difficult to concentrate if my back is cramping, my legs have fallen asleep, and I'm shivering.

Inside the tent, my big eleven-pound (nearly five-kilogram), 600-millimeter telephoto lens and digital SLR camera sit in front of me on a sturdy tripod with a hefty ball head. The lens points at the nest through a draw-corded sleeve in the front of the blind.

I keep an additional camera body at my side. Extra batteries warm in my parka pocket. In another pocket I keep a bag of gorp handy, my food in the field. My field notebook lies next to me, open and ready for quick note taking.

From inside I peer out through small window slits covered in camouflage netting. This allows me to monitor the owls and the area around the nest, all without them seeing me. I avoid making sudden movements or noise—the parent owls are very sensitive to all that goes on around their nest.

Life in my hideout usually moves at a slow pace. Often I sit for hours, waiting for something to happen at the nest. I liken my sit in the blind to photographing a Red Sox baseball game from the first base photographer's pit at Fenway Park, which I often did as a staff photographer for the *Boston Globe*.

For me, a baseball game was usually eight innings of boredom punctuated by—if I was lucky—an inning's worth of action. I better not be snoozing when the action breaks, whether it's a grand slam over Fenway Park's Green Monster or a brilliant male snowy owl on a fastball approach to the nest, a lemming in his talons.

When the female looks off into the distance, raising her head, staring and maybe head bobbing, I perk up. The male is probably en route, winging toward the nest for a food drop.

Denver had cautioned me that the male would land at the nest mound, hand off the lemming, and then be gone within five to ten seconds. Anticipating where the male will land at the nest is tricky, though following the direction of the female's stare helps.

And then suddenly the male wings into view, several hundred feet (more than a hundred meters) behind the nest. He's flying low and fast, his 4.5-foot-long (1.37-meter-long) wings practically brushing the tundra. I pick him up in my camera viewfinder and engage the autofocus. The camera tracks his rapid approach. I begin clicking photos at twelve frames per second.

In a few moments, the brilliant white male lands on the edge of the nest mound, a fat brown lemming dangling from his beak. He steps toward the female as she scuttles to him. With eyes closed, he leans forward, offering her the lemming, which she practically yanks from his beak. He stands up, looks around, and then vaults into the air, winging off to hunt for another lemming. He's been at the nest for seven seconds. A snowy owl parent's work is never done.

Neither is the work of a snowy owl researcher.

CHAPTER 7
THE OWL CHICK HEIST

One day in early August 1998, fourteen-year-old Nagruk Harcharek and his two friends—Jonas Ahsoak and Jens Hopson, both fifteen—decided to go duck hunting. They grabbed their shotguns and hopped onto two ATVs and sped off, eventually leaving the gravel road by the Distant Early Warning Line radar station and driving across the tundra, headed for the shoreline of Brant Point.

From the beach they had a good view over the shallow bay and could easily spot the long wavering lines of migrating king eiders skimming low over the water. Sometimes the big eider flocks flared up and over the boys, speeding past overhead.

By late afternoon, they had bagged several eiders. They packed up and started for home, retracing their route over the tundra from earlier in the day.

On the way out to Brant Point, they

← Denver instructs Nagruk on how to band a snowy owl chick that Nagruk and his friends had taken off the tundra the day before. Nagruk is wearing a sealskin hat that his mother sewed for him.

had noticed fuzzy owl chicks hunkering in the grasses and lichens, waiting for their parents to bring in a lemming. But it wasn't until the return trip that the boys decided they would catch the baby owls, bring them home, and keep them as pets. "That was our grandiose idea between us," recalls Nagruk, years later.

The boys gathered up the three chicks, placing two of them into a bag and tucking the third chick under Jens's jacket.

At Jonas's house they loaded the owl chicks into a Rubbermaid storage tote. The young owls were hungry, so the boys fed them some caribou meat and lunch meat they found in the fridge. Jonas propped the lid of the tote open with a stick so the owl chicks would have fresh air.

The next morning, Jonas's mother, Eunice Akpik, heard noises coming from the container and noticed the stick propping the lid open. She peeked in and three fuzzy gray owl chicks glared up at her. She let out a startled holler and quickly shut the lid.

↑ From the warmth of his parka, Denver extracts one of the two snowy owl chicks returned to the tundra.

↑ The two chicks, back on their home turf.

She scolded Jonas, asking him how the baby owls had ended up in their house. Next she called the local veterinary office. The vet came out, collected the owl chicks, and after consulting with the Wildlife Department, brought them to Denver—whose field office that year happened to be in the same building as the Wildlife Department.

Many years after the chick heist, Nagruk explained to me by phone call from Utqiagvik what happened next.

"Denver's initial thought was we needed to get these chicks back out to their parents, wherever they are, but he had no idea where we'd gotten them from, nor did my friend's mom. She knew who Jonas was with at the time. Everybody thought they were going to get in trouble so nobody wanted to fess up until Denver got ahold of my mom.

"I remember [my mom] came to my room and she woke me up and she was not happy and said, 'You need to get your you-know-what out of bed, because you're going to help these guys bring these owls back.' So, I didn't have much of a choice.

"I got up and I geared up and I got on my four-wheeler and

← Nagruk and Denver place the captured snowy owl chicks back on the tundra near their nest.

I met with Denver and Daniel Cox [a wildlife photographer] out at the Arctic Research Facility at the Naval Arctic Research Laboratory.

"Denver made me feel really comfortable as far as helping him out, telling me, 'You're not in trouble and we just need your help in getting these chicks back out to their parents.' He gave me the spiel on owls and how difficult it would be raise one in captivity and how it's not a really good idea. It was a very educational experience on many levels.

"So, then it turned into 'We're going to take the chicks [to where you found them] and we want you to help us band them.'

"We put [the owl chicks] in a small dog kennel and loaded them onto the ATV and Denver and Dan followed me. We went to the exact same spot where we picked them up, and the parents were still around," said Nagruk.

Denver had worried the chicks' parents wouldn't still be in the area. Luckily, the teenagers had missed picking up one of the snowy owl chicks. The parents were still near the nest, feeding the lone baby.

Denver and Nagruk banded the three chicks and then set them back on the tundra. The chicks put their heads down and ran a short distance and then stopped to look back at Nagruk and Denver.

The chicks stretched and flapped. Within minutes the parents were flying overhead, barking their concern at the humans near their babies. The family was reunited. In the process, a lasting friendship between Denver and Nagruk was kindled.

Nagruk went on to become the general manager for UIC Science and a vice president of UIC lands. He earned a commercial pilot's license and flies his own Cessna 182.

In 2014, Denver and Nagruk traipsed back onto the tundra to band snowy owl chicks not far from the spot where as a teenager Nagruk and his friends had scooped up the owl chicks all those years ago.

An adult snowy owl circled the men as they banded, and then he flew in, nailing Nagruk in the back.

"I figure it was retribution," says Nagruk, laughing.

What to Do If You Find an Injured Owl

While snowy owls rarely get injured by vehicle strikes in Utqiagvik, in most of the United States and large parts of Canada, many owls and hawks are injured or killed when they collide with moving vehicles.

If you find an injured or stunned owl by the side of the road, you can help the bird and perhaps save its life. First, make sure you aren't going to be struck by traffic as you help the owl. Check that your car is parked safely out of the line of traffic. If your owl rescue happens at night, make sure you use lights. Try to have a light-colored or reflective jacket at hand so you can slip it on to help drivers see you.

If you happen to have leather work gloves handy, put them on to protect your hands. If you don't have gloves available, that's okay. Next, find a coat or blanket that you can put over the injured raptor. Once the bird is covered, gently wrap the coat or blanket loosely around the bird. Then carefully but firmly grasp the bird (keeping the blanket between your hands and its body), making sure that the bird's legs and feet are pointed down and away from you. A raptor's powerful feet and sharp talons can injure you if you don't pick it up properly.

If you have a cardboard box, place the bird into it. Try to uncover the bird before you close the box. Make sure there are air holes in the box so the bird can get fresh air. If you don't have a box, you can place the bird in your trunk unless it's a hot day. As a last resort you can place the bird, still wrapped in the coat or blanket, on the floor of your car.

You'll need to transport the bird to a wildlife clinic, wildlife rehab facility, or a veterinarian that treats wildlife. Don't try to feed or give water to the injured bird. While it's legal to transport an injured raptor to a clinic, it's not legal for you to try to treat the bird yourself. Doctors and rehabbers are legally licensed to treat wildlife.

Every spring, it happens. People discover a flightless

↑ Marcia Wilson helps a Massachusetts homeowner put up a temporary nest platform for a great horned owl chick that prematurely fell from it's nest, located higher up in the same tree.

owl chick on their lawn or perched on a low branch in their yard or neighborhood. With no parent owls in sight, most people might conclude the owl needs to be rescued. Wrong!

Most likely the baby owl has just left the nest on its first attempt to fly, or the owl fell out because she lost her balance. Perhaps the chick was knocked out of the nest by a sibling or a gust of wind. If the chick is extremely young (in which case you won't see any long flight feathers growing on the wings), then you can build a second "nest" with some adult assistance. A plastic basin or open-topped wood box attached to a simple wood-framed platform can serve as a

→ Marcia picks up the young chick to place it in its new nest.

temporary nest. Place it at least six feet (about two meters) up on a tree trunk. Drill some small drainage holes in the basin. Throw several handfuls of pine shavings in the bottom. Place the baby in its new nest. Rest assured that the parents are nearby and will continue to feed the chick.

If the chick is larger but can't fly, you might put on gloves and gently clasp the chick's body from above (holding the wings firmly to the body with your gentle grip) and put the chick onto a branch perch four or five feet (about one and a half meters) off the ground. Then keep the family cat or dog away from that area for a few days. The owl parents will continue to feed the growing chick.

Don't worry about the urban legend that says handling a baby bird will cause its parents to smell your scent on the

baby and reject it. Not true. While many birds have a sense of smell, in some birds it doesn't seem to be well developed. And with most any bird, the parent won't reject its baby just because you handled it.

On a scent-related note: If you find a bird's nest, don't approach it closely, because the scent trail you leave may lead a raccoon, opossum, skunk, or other ground predator to the nest. While raptors usually defend against nest predations, most non-raptors (such as songbirds and ducks) can't stop predators from eating eggs or chicks.

In the case of a snowy owl nest, the male regularly fends off arctic foxes, so Denver need not worry about the scent trail he leaves around the owl's nest. Besides, there are no raccoons, opossums, or skunks in the Arctic.

CHAPTER 8
STRIKE UP THE BANDS

On a fine tundra day in late July, Denver and Liberty set out to check all four snowy owl nests, find the wandering owl chicks, and tag them with numbered aluminum bracelets called bands.

Snowy owl chicks leave the nest when they are about twenty-one days old. They can't fly yet, but wanderlust grips these tundra butterballs, their white and brown adult feathers erupting through their gray juvenile down coats.

The parent owls keep close track of their wayward chicks. The male owl begins feeding them directly, a task the female hasn't allowed him to do until now. Once all the chicks leave the nest, the female will join the hunt, both she and the male scouring the tundra to capture lemmings for their always hungry, rapidly growing youngsters.

"Okay, Liberty, why don't you head over in that area to search for chicks," says Denver, waving his arm toward a swath of hillocky tundra with lots of dips and pockets where a baby owl could crouch to hide.

"I'll search back over here," says Denver, nodding over his shoulder toward another expanse of lumpy tundra.

Denver hasn't walked far when Liberty calls out, "Got one!" She carries the fluffy gray lump back to the nest mound and deposits it there. Once a chick is in hand, it doesn't struggle. Holding a chick requires a steady, slightly firm—but not tight—two-handed grip. When tucked up against one's fleece jacket, a chick remains calm and quiet. Liberty walks off, continuing her search.

Meanwhile, the protective father snowy owl is glaring and barking at us from above. Liberty and Denver try to keep tabs on the male's whereabouts as they search for other chicks, but it's a bit distracting knowing who wheels overhead with needle talons on his big feet and family protection on his mind.

Moments later, a muffled exclamation comes from Liberty's direction. She's lying facedown on the tundra. The

← Before Denver and Liberty can band snowy owl chicks, they have to find them as the chicks explore the tundra around their nest mound.

male snowy owl has just whacked her backpack, raking his talons across it. Luckily Liberty saw him coming at the last moment and hit the deck. She gets up, looking a bit frazzled.

A few minutes later, the male comes for Denver. Ever the seasoned researcher and athlete, Denver coolly eyes the incoming owl and at the last second feints left. The brilliant white male whizzes past, just missing him. Denver watches him go, looking unperturbed and focused.

Denver notes that such aggressive males make excellent parents because they are such stalwart defenders of their nest and chicks. Denver could just as easily have been an arctic fox looking for an easy meal of owl chick. That fox would go away hungry if that was the case here, as the male snowy owl would quickly and efficiently turn it away.

Denver continues to search for chicks, walking concentric rings around the nest and closely watching for movement on the tundra that indicates a chick has spotted him. Once a chick sees him, it often lowers its head and takes off running.

Or Denver might spy a mushroom-like mound of feathers flattened on the tundra—a crouching owl chick that's trying to hide.

Sometimes Denver can locate a chick by observing the aggressiveness of a protective male: The closer Denver wanders to the hidden chick, the closer the male flies, readying a defensive attack.

"Got another one," quips Liberty. She's proving to be a sharp-eyed owl chick locator. At more than one nest she finds all four or five chicks in short order. The part of chick searching that she never gets used to is the sudden attacks from male snowy owls defending the nest.

More than once Liberty threw herself into a hasty

→ Denver hoots to a male snowy owl circling overhead, ready to defend his chicks against human interveners.

face-plant as a speeding male snowy owl attacked from behind, suddenly strafing her. Each time, Liberty's backpack took the brunt of the talon strike, and yet we could tell her nerves were fraying from multiple assaults.

Chicks who are at least twenty-one days old are ready for banding. A number 8 band is an aluminum bracelet inscribed with a unique identification number. The band also lists an address where you can report the band number in case you recover or sight a banded bird.

Bands are issued by the United States Geological Survey's Bird Banding Lab in Patuxent, Maryland. Each year Denver

→ "Got one!" says Liberty, holding the first chick of four she found. Note that this chick wears a band from a previous banding day.

↑ Liberty hits the tundra as a male snowy owl strikes her backpack while defending his chicks who are wandering nearby.

→   Sitting on their nest mound, six snowy owl chicks rest while Denver prepares to band them.

submits his banding records to the lab, which maintains a giant database of millions of banded birds of hundreds of species.

Before Denver begins banding the babies, he likes to bring the wandering chicks back to the nest mound. There he sits with the chicks gathered at his feet. One by one he works his way through the downy crowd of babies, giving each one a bright, shiny leg band.

Though most bird banders place a band on the bird's right leg, Denver prefers to band snowy owls on the left leg, perhaps owing to his slight rebel scientist streak.

Banding owl chicks is easier with two people. Liberty

Denver's daypack contains all the things he needs to conduct his field research.

lightweight day pack

sunscreen

mosquito head net

assorted spring scales

#8 and #9 aluminum owl bands and band pliers

compass

rangefinder to determine distances

handheld GPS unit

data notebook for each snowy owl nest

sunglasses

metallized tarp for emergency warmth

photocopied topographic map of owl study area

hand sanitzer

close-up glasses

water bottle

thermometer

food – gorp, dried mango, salmon jerky

small envelopes for feather samples

felt tip pens

field notebook with pens

sealable plastic bags for large feathers and pellets

not shown: toilet paper

While sheltering in the lee of the nest mound, Liberty holds the chick as Denver places a band on the bird's left leg.

↑ A string of aluminum bands and pliers stand at the ready for banding snowy owl chicks.

↑ These twenty-one-day-old chicks quietly wait from a comfortable perch on Liberty's boots as Denver prepares to band them.

holds the young owls while Denver uses pliers to crimp the number 8 lock-on band on each chick's leg.

Banding an owl doesn't hurt it, though Denver is careful to make sure the band isn't too tight and doesn't have any sharp edges that could abrade the owl's leg. The owl will wear the band for the rest of its life. And while Denver hopes to band all the chicks from each nest, sometimes a chick or two will prove elusive.

Every bird bander dreams of band recoveries. Denver notes that even though band returns are infrequent, when he does get one, "it always reveals something really interesting about the owl."

With the advent of birders' and wildlife photographers' widespread use of digital cameras and sharp telephoto lenses,

bands on many species can be read from photos of perched or free-flying birds by enlarging the image. Banding returns come from afar, or sometimes from the same area the bird was banded in a previous year. Alas, reports for banded snowy owls have been scant. Part of the explanation for this lies with the thick feathers that grow all the way down a snowy owl's leg. A leg band that's buried beneath those feathers may be impossible to see.

Bird banding is just one more arrow in the quiver of tools that scientists use to slowly untangle and discover bird movements. And as Liberty discovered, it's a good excuse to hold an incredibly soft snowy owl chick in your lap. Better yet, make that two incredibly soft chicks.

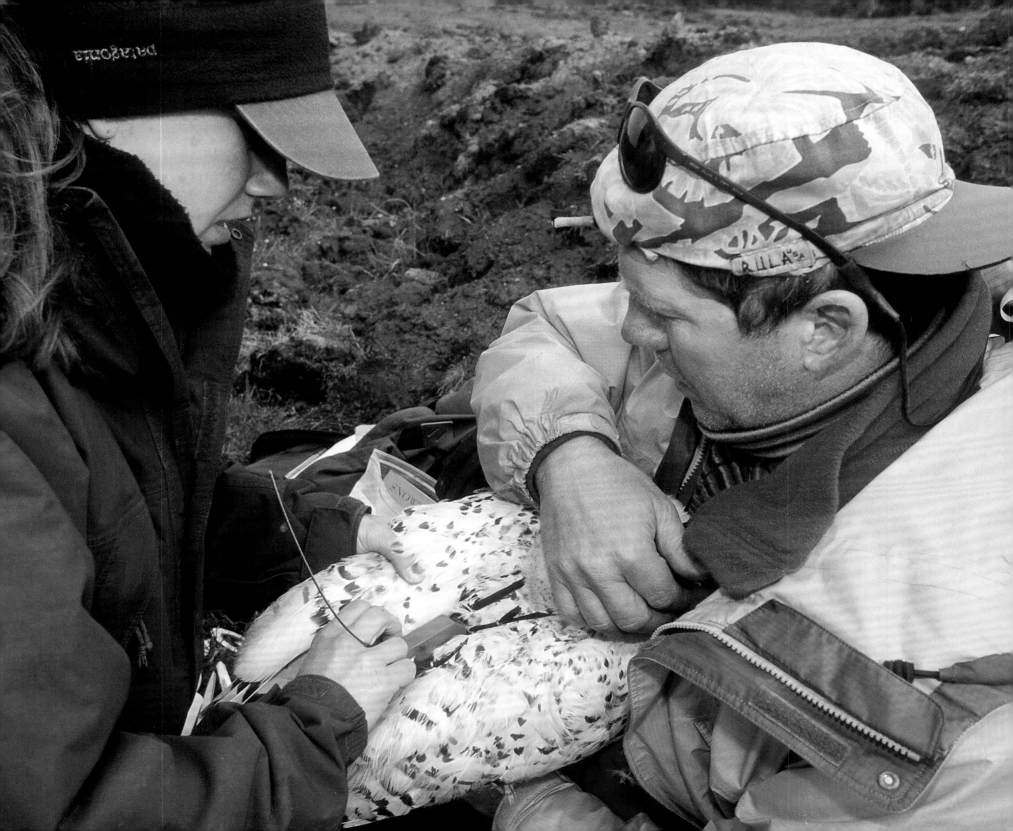

CHAPTER 9
TRACKING OWLS

To track a snowy owl, you first have to catch a snowy owl.

During the summer of 1999, Denver was figuring out how to do just that so he could attach a satellite transmitter to an owl. If he succeeded, it would be the first snowy owl in the world to be tracked by satellite. Denver had no doubts the transmitter would reveal a remarkable travel story that until then would have been unknowable. First, Denver had to catch a snowy owl. But how?

One of Denver's early attempts at capturing an adult owl involved a noose carpet—a backing screen covered with scores of monofilament nooses that, in theory, would slip over the owl's foot and entangle the leg when the owl stepped onto the carpet. The entangling nooses would prevent the owl from escaping.

Noose carpets or similar traps called bal-chatri traps have long been used by falconers to catch raptors they intend to train as hunting birds.

Denver had the ingenious idea of attaching a noose carpet to the back of his parka. He would then approach the nest of an owl pair where he knew the male to be an aggressive defender of the chicks.

Knowing that the male owl would come at him from behind, Denver figured if he lay down next to the nest, the male might strike him on the back, where the noose carpet was attached. If all went according to plan, the owl would get entangled and suddenly Denver would have a bundle of flailing talons and flapping wings attached to his back. An assistant would rush in and secure the owl.

The noose-carpet parka didn't work. The nest-defending male struck Denver's back, but the nooses never snared the owl's feet.

Next, Denver decided to mount a noose carpet on a screen of hardware cloth that he spiked down into the soil at a nest with an egg. Denver didn't want the female owl to fly away

← While Denver (right) holds the female snowy owl, Laura fits the transmitter harness onto the bird.

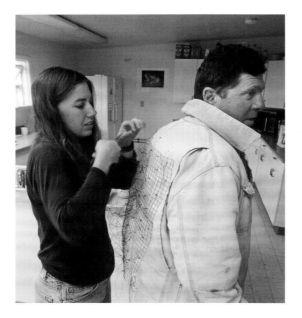

↑ Denver and Laura lay out a noose carpet at a snowy owl nest. Note the lemming on the carpet next to the egg.

with the noose carpet, so he had to make sure it was securely anchored to the ground.

Denver removed all the lemmings he found at the nest. After pulling one lemming aside, he laid it and the egg on the noose carpet.

From a blind a few hundred feet (about ninety meters) away, Denver watched the female owl return to the nest. She looked around and saw no lemmings, except for the one draped across the noose carpet. She walked onto the carpet to reach for the lemming and her foot became entangled. Denver and his research assistant Laura Phillips quickly moved in, calmly securing the female.

Next, he and Laura readied a harness that would hold the lightweight satellite transmitter. They took care in fitting the harness to the owl, knowing that it couldn't be so tight that it would cause chafing, or so loose that it would fall off. The transmitter weighed less than two ounces (fifty-seven grams)—not a significant load for a two-and-a-half-pound (just-over-one-kilogram) owl.

The female owl was soon sitting back on her nest, sporting a new satellite transmitter. Over the next several months her transmitter would send weekly uploads of her location to a computer in Idaho. He would get printed reports showing where the owl had been. Denver would have first eyes on the travelogue of a Barrow-nesting snowy owl who was on the move after the nesting season.

Also in 1999, Denver placed a satellite transmitter on another nesting female snowy owl. By March of 2000, both owls had traveled across the Chukchi Sea and entered Russia somewhere near the Bering Strait. Both spent the summer of

2000 along the northern coast of Siberia within view of the Arctic Ocean. Denver wondered if they nested, though he had no way of knowing.

By July 2001, both females had arrived on Victoria Island in Canada's Northwest Territories. And again, Denver wondered if they were nesting.

"We were the first researchers to put satellite transmitters on snowy owls. Since then the technology has advanced. Now it's much better," says Denver. Modern transmitters upload GPS data to cell phone towers whenever they are within range rather than uploading to a satellite. Batteries now recharge by tiny solar panel on the transmitter, powering the data collection for years to come. The transmitter harnesses are now designed to eventually fall off.

"But I'm at the point where we need to get beyond the 'Gee whiz' reaction to tracking owls," says Denver. "We need to know what these birds are doing when they show up on Victoria Island. Are they nesting? Is the lemming population peaking? We need to go there and see what's happening."

Denver's dream would be to oversee a team of researchers traveling to all the circumpolar tundra areas to count snowy owls and determine if they are nesting, and to assess lemming populations. Denver notes that this census would need to be conducted over several summers. The logistics for such surveys? Daunting. The cost to conduct multiyear field studies? Breathtaking.

And yet, the idea of these far-flung surveys continues to inhabit Denver's thoughts. One senses that if Denver could find funding for the multiyear surveys, he would find a way to marshal the field researchers to get it done.

↑ Denver gets ready to release the female snowy owl who's wearing the backpack transmitter. Note the antenna sticking out from her back.

Tracking Snowy Owls

Where do snowy owls go when they leave Utqiagvik? To find out, Denver attached satellite transmitters to four snowy owls (females #1 and #2 in 1999, females #3 and #4 in 2000).

Female #1 (see map 1) spent time along the Alaskan coast before she beelined for Russia, hitting land on the north coast and then flying southward, and later north. She summered at the coast. Nesting? Denver couldn't confirm it. The following year (map 2) she came back to Utqiagvik before she peeled off, ending up on Banks Island in Canada for the summer. Nesting? Maybe.

Female #2 (map 1) flew south over the sea and lingered two and a half months around Alaska's St. Lawrence Island. She too summered on the north Siberian coast. Nesting? Good question. She wintered in Russia, then the following year (map 2) she too came back to Utqiagvik before flying east and then north to Victoria Island, which neighbors Banks Island.

Female # 3 (map 2) wintered on the coast of southeast Alaska before she headed north to spend the summer of 2001 on Victoria Island. That year female #4 also summered on Banks Island, not far from female #1. Nesting? That's anybody's guess.

The snowy owl study area map (at far right) depicts some of the area's complex biodiversity, and who's on the menu for hungry snowy owls.

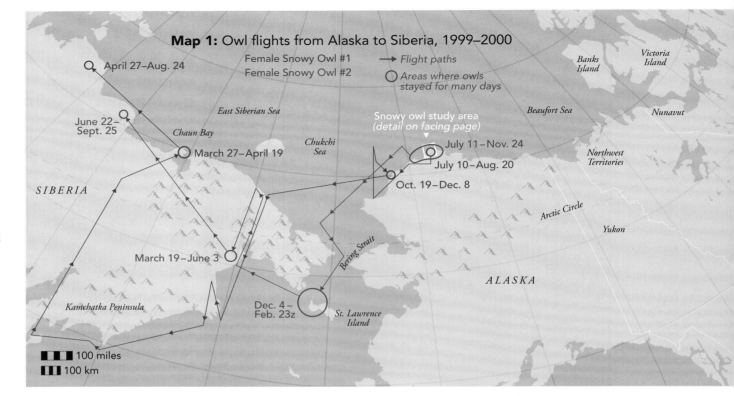

Map 1: Owl flights from Alaska to Siberia, 1999–2000

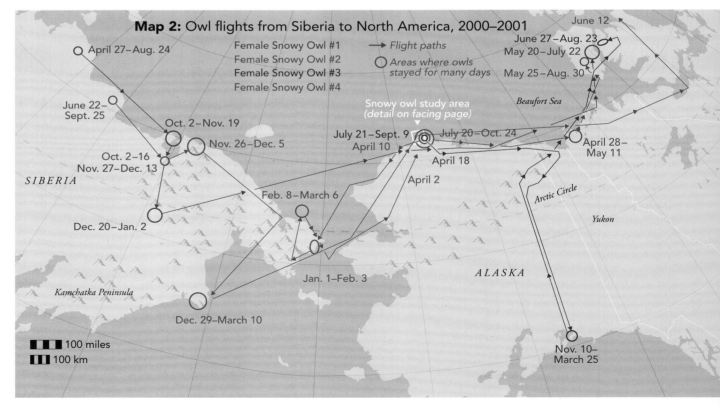

Map 2: Owl flights from Siberia to North America, 2000–2001

CHAPTER 10
THE NOMADS DEPART

Imagine trying to fly a hang glider for the first time after only watching others in action. Tough to do! Your first flights would be short hops. Landings might involve low-speed crashes. The longer you practiced, the better you'd get at flying.

By late August, most of the snowy owl chicks who left their nests are able to fly. Their first flights aren't pretty or graceful. The young owls exercise their wings, flapping vigorously to strengthen flight muscles and build coordination. The youngsters face a time crunch: They must learn to fly well enough to move south, off the tundra, before harsh weather returns in September.

Denver usually leaves Utqiagvik by mid-August, returning to his home base in Montana. Nomadic young snowy owls aren't far behind.

In the northern tier states of the contiguous United States, late-fall and winter influxes of snowy owls garner attention on television and in newspapers, also generating excited comments on social media. Most of the owls who arrive there are the young of the year, having hatched in late June or early July. Older snowy owls, particularly all-white males, tend to stay north of the lower forty-eight states, wintering instead in Canada, Alaska, or even Russia.

Sometimes many young owls show up in the eastern United States while other parts of the country see few. Other winters, the Midwest hits the jackpot. The Pacific Northwest might see droves of these ghostly visitors when few are to be seen in the Midwest or New England.

Where I live in Massachusetts, at least a few snowy owls turn up every winter. Some years we see many, though we are rarely inundated.

In the winter of 2013–14, the eastern United States experienced a historically large flight of snowy owls. Hundreds passed into New England. The Audubon Christmas Bird Count on Nantucket tallied thirty-three on the island. One had even made its way to Little Talbot Island in northeastern

→ Some older, all-white, male snowy owls stay in the Arctic during the winter, perhaps to remain near nesting territories they will use in spring. The thick, dense feathers of snowy owls allow them to endure temperatures of –50 degrees F (-45 degrees C.).

Florida, only the state's third record for this species.

Another had navigated to Bermuda, where it was photographed sitting on the roof of a pink house. Unfortunately, that owl died after eating poisoned rats.

Foreshadowing that winter influx, large numbers of nesting owls were found in northern Quebec on the Ungava Peninsula in the summer of 2013. At each nest, male owls were delivering scores of lemmings—even before the chicks had hatched. One memorable photo that still circulates online shows seventy lemming and eight vole carcasses ringing a nest that holds three eggs and one newly hatched chick.

The following fall and winter, a bumper crop of young snowy owls started showing up south of Quebec. Norman

Smith, an owl researcher and raptor bander, as well as a colleague and friend of Denver's, banded 121 of them at Logan International Airport in Boston, Massachusetts. He's been relocating snowy owls from there since 1981 as part of his job as sanctuary director for Massachusetts Audubon Society's Blue Hills Trailside Museum.

Snowy owls that end up at Logan are lucky, because Norman live traps them with a baited bow trap, bands them, and releases them at food-rich sites on the North and South Shores of Massachusetts, away from the busy airport. Many large metropolitan airports in the United States shoot owls because they present a hazard for aircraft.

Norman banded fifty-eight additional owls in Massachusetts that winter, away from the airport. Weights of these owls show them to be healthy, and not starving. Only a tiny percentage (<1%) of the snowy owls arriving in the state are underweight according to Norman's data.

Other owl banders across the lower forty-eight states also find first year snowy owl weights to be healthy. The data are clear: starving snowy owls are the exception, not the rule.

All of these regional winter influxes suggest that somewhere in the Arctic, north of that US region, snowy owls had a highly successful summer breeding season. It also means there were lots of lemmings for the owls to eat.

Young snowy owls disperse far and wide, turning up in some surprising places. In 2013, a lone snowy owl was spotted at the airport in Honolulu, Hawaii. And, yes, this bird met the same fate as other owls at New York's JFK and LaGuardia airports

→ Norman Smith releases a banded snowy owl with help from his granddaughters. The owl was live-trapped at Logan Airport in Boston and released on a beach on the South Shore of Massachusetts.

← A solar-powered GSM transmitter (visible on the owl's back) uploads GPS data through a cell tower connection, allowing researchers to precisely track the owl's movements. This female snowy owl was live-trapped in March at Boston's Logan International Airport by Norman Smith, who banded her, attached the backpack transmitter, and released her on a salt marsh south of Boston. The owl flew to Baffin Island in the Canadian Arctic the following summer. The public can track snowy owls wearing transmitters on the website www.projectsnowstorm.org.

and New Jersey's Newark Liberty International Airport—he was shot.

Snowy owls don't always migrate according to expected timetables. In 2017, at least five summered along coastal Massachusetts instead of moving northward in late March or April as most Massachusetts-wintering snowy owls do, staying far south of their expected summer range in the Arctic. Two of them stayed over to the following winter. Two succumbed to poisoning from rodenticides, while the third summering owl died from complications of a parasite infection, according to Norman.

In the eastern United States, wintering snowy owls occur in greater numbers at the coast than they do inland. Researchers believe one reason for this is the abundance of prey the owls find there. Compared to their Arctic diets, there is a veritable smorgasbord of mammals, birds, fish, and even carrion for owls along the coast. I've watched snowy owls hunt tiny Savannah sparrows in Massachusetts salt marshes and dunes.

At the other extreme of prey size, Norman saw a Logan Airport snowy owl take down a great blue heron in flight, kill it, and then devour part of it. He also watched a big female owl feeding on the carcass of another snowy owl, which he believes she killed; days earlier he had watched her aggressively attack other snowy owls at the airport.

Norman's list of prey consumed by snowy owls wintering in Massachusetts at the airport is hugely varied and often surprising. He has seen them take an array of raptors, including long-eared owls, short-eared owls, barred owls, barn owls, northern harriers, American kestrels, and peregrine falcons.

His list includes various sandpipers, plovers, clapper rails, starlings, and a host of other birds. Norman was surprised to see a snowy owl feeding on the meats of washed-up blue mussels (a shellfish) and fish.

The coastal winter menu commonly includes waterfowl such as Canada geese, common eiders, black ducks, mallards, common goldeneyes, urban Norway rats, the occasional free-ranging cat, and gulls. Make that lots of gulls, though it's mostly the smaller ones, such as ring-billed gulls and Bonaparte's gulls that make up the menu.

Wintering snowy owls have the option of hunting in darkness as opposed to the twenty-four-hour daylight imposed on them on the Arctic nesting grounds. When food is abundant, the owls seem to favor nocturnal hunting. When food is scarce or bad weather makes hunting difficult, they will hunt day and night. They can often be crepuscular, hunting at twilight.

While the snowy owls that show up in winter in the lower forty-eight states aren't starving, it's perhaps no surprise that they gravitate to the wide-open habitats that support lots of prey. Wouldn't you too like to hang out for the winter at the all-you-can-eat buffet?

CHAPTER 11
A WARMING ARCTIC

Climatologists and meteorologists have warned for decades that the Arctic is warming about twice as fast as other parts of the planet.

Cycles of warming and cooling have occurred across the Arctic for millennia, but those changes took place over thousands or tens of thousands of years. The recent accelerated Arctic warming is occurring over the course of a few decades—a mere blink of time on a geological timescale. Scientists cite the burning of fossil fuels and the escape of carbon dioxide and methane from thawing tundra as prime drivers of this accelerated warming.

Permafrost is melting, causing ocean-facing tundra to erode and slough into the sea. Rising sea levels from melting glaciers in Greenland and the Antarctic ice cap, coinciding with the early melting and late formation of sea ice in the Arctic, accelerates the beach erosion. Many low-lying coastal

← Large bags of sand placed atop a man-made dune of sand and gravel attempt to hold back the hungry Chukchi Sea surf from one of Utqiagvik's key coastal roads.

villages in the Alaskan Arctic face more frequent flooding during storms. In some settlements, houses are starting to slump or tip as the permafrost under them melts.

In Utqiagvik, parts of Point Barrow have already disappeared into the sea. Toward town, the community has dumped thousands of yards (meters) of sand and gravel to build a man-made dune to keep waves from overwashing its coastal roads. On other parts of the shoreline, where man-made barrier dunes and natural bluffs face the sea, giant black or white sandbags placed at their base stave off a hungry surf—for now.

Melting permafrost under inland tundra releases trapped methane, which is a greenhouse gas eighty-four times more potent than carbon dioxide at warming the earth. As more permafrost melts, more methane and carbon dioxide will be released to our atmosphere, causing yet more warming.

What does this warming mean for the Arctic's plants and animals? Changes are afoot as shrubs and trees move

northward in a warmer climate. Rainfall patterns are changing, with some areas becoming wetter (Utqiagvik, perhaps) and other areas becoming drier.

Diminished sea ice means more water can evaporate in the warmer summers, causing thunderstorms to become more frequent. Lightning strikes can ignite remote tundra, causing fires, which were once nearly unheard of in much of the Arctic. Diminished sea ice also means the darker water will heat up more quickly than if sunlight was reflecting off ice.

Disappearing sea ice leaves hungry polar bears stranded on shore, where they can't hunt for seals. In July and August, some bears at Utqiagvik gnaw on the bowhead whale carcasses that the village hunt produced in April and May. The pickings are lean. Some bears try to find bird nests to raid a few eggs, but that can't replace a fat-rich, calorie-dense diet of seal. A bear may wander into town and cause trouble, trying to scavenge garbage out of dumpsters.

Snowy owls face an uncertain future at Utqiagvik. Denver's data points to a long, slow decline in the number nesting there. Teasing the data apart to yield its secrets is tricky and complicated.

↑   A polar bear walks the beach at Point Barrow, scavenging what little food it can find. Bones from bowhead whales that were harvested by the community in April are visible behind the bear.

← At the nest, Denver examines a one- or two-day-old chick whose eyes have yet to open."

owls. He does know that lemmings are his reliable indicator species for assessing the tundra's faunal health and diversity. Are snowy owls finding it harder to catch enough lemmings to sustain nesting? This question will prove hard to answer.

While Denver tracks lemming populations and snowy owl nestings with long-term studies, his data offer no easy solutions for halting a snowy owl decline.

Part of the problem in assessing the status of snowy owls is that no one has a reliable world population estimate that's not based on assumptions and guesses with large margins of error.

In a sad, candid moment out on the tundra, Denver allows that Utqiagvik will probably lose the snowy owl as a nesting species. He can't say when that might happen, but I could tell that he thought it could occur in his lifetime, and he's in his midsixties.

Snowy owls and lemmings have been around for millions of years. Whether they are around for millions more may depend on what humanity accomplishes—or fails to accomplish—in this century.

Are fewer snowy owls nesting at Utqiagvik because of increased land use by human developments? Maybe. Consider that years ago the airport expanded onto what one older Inupiat described as tundra dense with nesting owls.

More people are building homes on pilings on expanses of tundra where Denver once studied snowy owls on nests.

And then there's the question of lemmings. Are populations of brown lemmings declining? Or are we on the cusp of such a decline? If so, why?

Denver readily concedes that he doesn't know if a warmer climate will help or hinder lemmings and nesting snowy

CHAPTER 12
WHAT YOU CAN DO

From your home in the lower forty-nine states or southern-tier Canadian provinces it's hard to know how you might help snowy owls and lemmings. One thing that you can do, wherever you live, is to look for snowy owls in the winter and come to appreciate the types of habitat they need to survive. Most states have records of snowy owls, with rare, surprising sightings coming from Florida, Texas, and even Hawaii. Northern-tier states see winter influxes of them much more frequently. The Canadian prairie provinces host snowy owls every winter. The Maritime provinces get their fair share in late fall and winter too.

Unlike Denver Holt, you should never approach a snowy owl closely. In the winter, snowy owls work hard to find food. Each time a person moves too close to one, causing it to fly, the owl burns precious calories. If several people flush the owl throughout the day, it may burn more calories than it can easily replace.

← A snow-covered brush pile offers potential shelter from predators for many animals including these gray squirrels.

To avoid causing an owl to fly off, use binoculars for your owl search. We've all heard of social distancing during the Covid-19 pandemic. Well, social distancing from wild owls is a good practice too. Just view your owl from several hundred feet (more than a hundred meters) away and use binoculars or a spotting scope for a closer look.

Suppose you want to take a photo of the snowy owl you've found and all you have is the camera in your phone. Try this: Focus your binoculars on the owl. Then line up the lens of your phone camera on the center of one of the eyepieces (the oculars). By carefully centering the camera lens on the ocular, you should be able to snap a photo that's post-worthy.

If you post an owl photo to social media, be general with information about where you found the owl. Revealing specific locations may draw too many people to the owl, causing it to repeatedly flush or leave the area.

One big way to help owls and the animals they eat is to avoid using rodenticides, those chemical poison baits that people often put out to kill mice and rats. Rodenticides don't kill their target right away, giving the poisoned mouse or rat time to escape. The sickened rodent makes an easy-to-catch meal for an owl, hawk, coyote, fox, or other predator. It's not hard to figure out where the rodenticide goes after an owl or hawk eats a poisoned mouse. It passes into the raptor, where it causes internal bleeding that could incapacitate or kill the bird.

Use snap traps baited with peanut butter as a safer and more humane way to rid your house or apartment of rodents. Plus, snap traps don't kill owls, hawks, or other carnivores that eat mice.

Lots of folks love a lush green lawn, yet few people seem to realize that the average lawn is a monoculture of grass, supporting little biodiversity. You might call it a wildlife desert (though deserts have higher species diversity than a lawn). In addition, lawns are resource hogs, consuming costly amounts of water, fertilizers, and chemical pesticides. If you are lucky enough to have a yard, consider keeping a portion of it wild to increase the species of plants and animals that might call your patch of land home. That means letting the grass grow along with the other plants that naturally start to take hold.

Don't treat your wild corner with insecticides, fertilizers, or weed killers. One option is to mow your the area but once a year, at the end of growing season. Another plan could be to not mow it at all, allowing shrubs and trees to sprout.

Branches from tree pruning or fallen branches from trees in the yard can be loosely stacked into a sheltering brush pile for insects, reptiles, amphibians, birds, and mammals. In my

→ A red eft spends a few years on land before changing into an aquatic eastern newt.

backyard brush pile I've seen white-footed mice, chipmunks, red squirrels, gray squirrels, weasels, mink, and wrens, cardinals, and blue jays, as well as a host of other birds using it for shelter from predators, a singing perch, a spot to forage for insects, or a place to rest.

Your wild place will attract a variety of insects and spiders, maybe frogs and salamanders, toads and turtles, and snakes—all indicator species of a healthy habitat.

Bird diversity will increase around your patch of wildness as they find more to eat and places to shelter and possibly nest (maybe in your brush pile). Though you might not see them, nocturnal mammals will start to feed in or live under your rough place in the yard in burrows. Diurnal mammals like chipmunks and squirrels will pass through. You might even attract nocturnal screech owls, barred owls, or the snowy owl's close relative the great horned owl to your wild and woolly backyard habitat. Mice and squirrels beware!

Finally, follow new research and seek out ideas about

how you can reduce your carbon footprint. That might mean walking or riding a bike instead of taking a car ride to a local destination, or helping your parents increase the weather stripping around doors and windows so your home is more energy efficient. Replace incandescent light bulbs with energy-efficient LED bulbs. Small efforts by many people can add up to make big differences in the amount of carbon dioxide our lifestyles release into the atmosphere.

If by chance you make it up to Utqiagvik to spy on lemmings and search for snowy owls, tell Denver that Mark sent you. And keep your binoculars handy!

↑ A tiger swallowtail nectars at blooms in a New England garden featuring plantings to attract hummingbirds, butterflies, bees, and other pollinators.

GLOSSARY

From the University of Alaska Fairbanks webpage glossary on correct word usage:

avinnaq—Inupiaq for "brown lemming."

Bubo scandiacus—genus and species scientific name for the snowy owl. *Bubo* means "horned owl." *Scandiacus* means "of Scandinavia."

circumpolar—the area around one of the earth's poles. The snowy owl has a circumpolar breeding range that rings the North Pole but does not extend up to it.

crepuscular—active in twilight.

diurnal—active during daylight.

Inupiak—used to refer to two of the indigenous people of Alaska.

Inupiaq—the language of Alaska Inuit spoken on the North Slope.

Inupiat—used to refer to three or more of the indigenous people of Alaska, to the people collectively, or to the culture. Never use "Inupiats."

Native—capitalize this when referring to people or individuals with ancestry in the indigenous peoples of Alaska.

nocturnal—active during darkness at night.

← A snowy owl sits out a blizzard at the coast of New Hampshire.

REFERENCES

Duncan, Dr. James R. *Owls of the World*. Buffalo, NY: Firefly Books, 2003.

Fuller, M., D. Holt, and L. Schueck. "Snowy Owl Movements: Variation on the Migration Theme." In *Avian Migration,* edited by P. Bertold, E. Gwinner, and E. Sonnenschein, pp. 359–66. Heidelberg, Germany: Springer-Verlag, 2003.

Holt, D. W. "Owls." In *Arctic Wings: Birds of the Arctic National Wildlife Refuge,* 112–26. Seattle: Mountaineers Books, 2006.

Holt, D. W., R. Berkley, C. Deppe, P. L. Enriquez-Rocha, P. D. Olsen, J. L. Petersen, J. L. Rangel-Salazar, K. P. Segars, and K. L. Wood. "Snowy Owl." In *Handbook of Birds of the World,* edited by J. del Hoyo, A. Elliott, and J. Sargatal, pp. 194–95. Barcelona: Lynx Edicions, 1999.

Holt, D. W., M. D. Larson, N. Smith, D. L. Evans, and D. F. Parmelee. "Snowy Owl *(Bubo scandiacus)*." In *The Birds of North America,* edited by P. G. Rodewald. Ithaca, NY: Cornell Lab of Ornithology, 2015.

Holt, D. W., M. T. Maples, J. L. Petersen-Parret, M. Korti, M. Seidensticker, and K. Gray. "Characteristics of Nest Mounds Used by Snowy Owls in Barrow, Alaska, with Conservation and Management Implications." *Ardea* 97, no. 4 (2009): 555–61.

MacLean, Edna Ahgeak. *Abridged Inupiaq and English Dictionary,* a joint publication of the Alaska Native Language Center, University of Alaska, Fairbanks, and the Inupiat Language Commission, North Slope Borough, Barrow, Alaska, 1981. https://uafanlc.alaska.edu/Online/IN(N)971M1981/maclean-1981-inupiaq_dictionary.pdf.

Seidensticker, Mathew T., Denver W. Holt, Jennifer Detienne, Sandra Talbot, and Kathy Gray. "Sexing Young Snowy Owls." *Journal of Raptor Research,* 45, no. 4 (2011): 281–89.

Webster, Donald H., and Wilfried Zibell. *Inupiat Eskimo Dictionary.* Fairbanks, AK: Summer Institute of Linguistics, 1970. https://library.alaska.gov/hist/hist_docs/docs/anlm/200078.pdf

Weidensaul, Scott. *Owls of North America and the Caribbean,* The Peterson Reference Guide Series. Boston: Houghton Mifflin Harcourt, 2015.

Owl Research Institute, https://www.owlresearchinstitute.org

Explore.org, https://explore.org/livecams/owl-research-institute/arctic-snowy-owl-nesting-cam

↑ An owl's eye is fixed in its socket, unable to roll up and down or left and right.

INDEX

SCIENTISTS IN THE FIELD

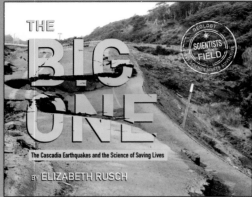

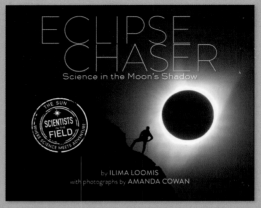

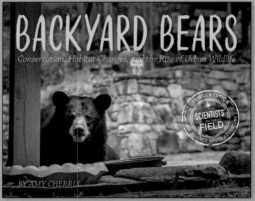

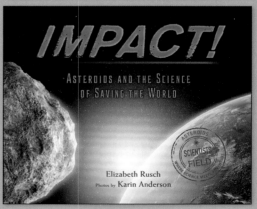

Where Science Meets Adventure

sciencemeetsadventure.com